Twayne's English Authors Series

Sylvia E. Bowman, *Editor*

INDIANA UNIVERSITY

William Godwin

(TEAS) 27

William Godwin

By ELTON EDWARD SMITH

University of South Florida

and ESTHER GREENWELL SMITH

Florida Southern College

Twayne Publishers, Inc.   ::   New York

MANUFACTURED IN THE UNITED STATES OF AMERICA

To DOROTHY DREW
Associate Professor, Syracuse University
Who introduced us to William Godwin

Preface

Forty-five years ago, B. Sprague Allen pointed out in an article in the *Publication of the Modern Language Association* that "Virtually all the current discussions of William Godwin devote the bulk of their attention to the elucidation of the anarchic social philosophy of his *Political Justice* (1793), and, as a rule, they give serious consideration to his first subsequent novel, *Caleb Williams* (1794). They deal perfunctorily and apologetically with *St. Leon* (1799), and generally refuse to extend their discussion beyond it so as to include *Fleetwood* (1805), *Mandeville* (1805), *Cloudesley* (1830), and *Deloraine* (1833)."

Today there seems to be no significant difference in the critical climate. Godwin is discussed peripherally in books on Shelley and his circle; or he is ignored as novelist, playwright, pamphleteer, biographer, and historian, and extolled as a radical political thinker in lieu of reading his radical political thought. In this volume, we have attempted to consider all his works and to relate our critical estimates to dominant themes; to do so, we have accumulated an unusually complete English, Godwin bibliography, although to meet the requirements of Twayne's English Authors Series we have eliminated all but a few critical studies; for these we have given brief evaluations.

Quite naturally, the major item in any Godwin study is the *Enquiry concerning Political Justice*, and Chapter 2 is devoted to an analysis of its shocking assertions, the total structure of its thought considered book by book, the relationships and cool logicality of the "shockers" when placed in the total structure, the derivations of Godwin's political philosophy, and its immediate effect of adulation and imitation, followed by a long period of vituperation.

Subsequent chapters deal with Godwin as pamphleteer, tractarian, and philosophical essayist, novelist, playwright, historian, biographer, and writer of books for children. No attempt is made to supply a complete life of Godwin or a gallery of contemporary portraits. Biographical and contemporaneous references are confined to the Chronology; to Chapter 1, "Introduction"; and to facts in other chapters which relate significantly to the motifs and production of his published works. There can be no serious question of the vast and fruitful influence of Godwin's thought, and this book attempts to analyze and present that thought.

We are grateful to all those who have assisted in the preparation of this study. The staffs of the University of South Florida Library, the Florida Southern College Library, the New York Public Library, and the Library of Congress have all been of the greatest help. Martha H. Covey and Dennis E. Robison managed to lure all the Godwin first editions to the new library at South Florida. Colleagues on our academic staffs have kept popping up with stray bits of information and mystification. The University of South Florida made possible several crucial trips to libraries in New York and Washington.

ELTON AND ESTHER SMITH

Lakeland, Florida

Contents

Preface

Chronology

1. Introduction   19
2. Political Theory   23
3. The Writer in Many Roles   54
4. Novels and Plays   84
5. History for Children and Adults   121
6. Conclusion   145

Notes and References   149

Selected Bibliography   159

Index   167

Chronology

1756 William Godwin born March 3, in Wisbeach, Cambridge-
shire, son of a Dissenting minister, seventh of thirteen
children.

1767 Placed with Mr. Samuel Newton, Calvinist preacher, at
Norwich, for private tutoring in a Classical education.

1771 Left Norwich, aged fifteen, to serve for several months as
usher in a small school run by his old master, Mr. Robert
Akers, at Hildolveston, near Guestwick.

1773 Following death of his father, November 12, 1772, came
to London, in April, with his mother, intending to enter
Homerton Academy. Rejected on suspicion of Sandemanianism; entered Hoxton College in September and remained five years.

1777 Last summer vacation in native county; preached at Yar-
mouth each Sunday morning and Lowestoft each afternoon. Candidated unsuccessfully for a pastorate at Christ-
church in Hampshire; settled as minister of the Dissenting
congregation at Ware in Hertfordshire, a Sandemanian in
theology, a Tory in politics.

1779 Left Ware in August and did not seek another charge,
but moved to London. Listened with admiration to the
speeches of Fox and Burke; exhausted his meager funds
and had to accept living at Stowmarket in Suffolk.

1781 Convinced by the political writings of Jonathan Swift and
by the Latin historians that monarchy was necessarily corrupt. Beginning of the erosion of his Toryism.

1782 Resigned living at Stowmarket over dispute on a minor
matter of church discipline. Faith shaken by Rousseau,
Holbach's *Système de la Nature,* and Helvétius' *De l'Esprit;*
doubted not only Calvinism, but the existence of God.

1783 Served as clergyman at Beaconsfield. Became Socinian from reading Priestley's *Institutes of Natural and Revealed Religion* and remained in this theological position until 1788. Wrote novel, *Damon and Delia*, in ten days; second novel, *Italian Letters*, in three weeks. *The History of the Life of William Pitt, Earl of Chatham*, published anonymously in London. *An Account of the Seminary that will be opened on Monday, the Fourth Day of August at Epsom in Surrey, for the Instruction of Twelve Pupils in the Greek, Latin, French, and English Languages*, pamphlet published anonymously by T. Cadell in London.

1784 Wrote novel, *Imogen, a Pastoral Romance*, January through April. Wrote *Sketches of History, in Six Sermons. The Herald of Literature* published anonymously.

1785 Contributed series of articles to new Whig review, *The Political Herald*, founded by Sheridan and his group. Declined editorship for fear membership in one party would limit his freedom of judgment. Wrote historical sections for the liberal *New Annual Register*, edited by his former tutor at Hoxton, Dr. Andrew Kippis.

1787- Conversations with Mr. Thomas Holcroft; became an un-
1800 believer in 1789; an atheist in 1792; a theist, in 1800, through the influence of Samuel Taylor Coleridge.

1791 Severed his connection with the *Register* on July 10, and with advances from Robinson the bookseller, began to write a treatise on political justice.

1793 January, published *An Enquiry concerning the Principles of Political Justice, and Its Influence on General Virtue and Happiness*, 8 volumes. Editions: London, 1793, 1796, 1798; Dublin, 1793; America, 1796.

1794 *Caleb Williams, Things as They Are: or, The Adventures of Caleb Williams*, 3 volumes. Editions: London, 1794, 1796, 1831, 1903, 1904; Paris, 1797. *Cursory Strictures on Lord Chief Justice Eyre's Charge to the Grand Jury*, pamphlet published anonymously.

1795 *Considerations on Lord Grenville's and Mr. Pitt's Bills*, pamphlet, by "A Lover of Order."

1797 *The Enquirer: Reflections on Education, Manners, and Literature*. Second edition, 1823. March 29, married Mary

Wollstonecraft (Imlay), who died September 10, after birth of Mary, August 30.

1798   *Memoirs of the Author of a Vindication of the Rights of Woman,* 4 volumes, edited anonymously by William Godwin.

1799   *St. Leon: a Tale of the Sixteenth Century,* 3 volumes. Editions: London, 1799, 1800, 1831, 1840; Paris, 1799; Dublin, 1800; Alexandria, Virginia, 1801.

1800   *Antonio: a Tragedy in Five Acts.* Autobiographical fragment of Godwin's early years to age fourteen (modelled on Rousseau's *Confessions*). July tour of Ireland.

1801   *Thoughts Occasioned by Dr. Parr's Spital Sermon,* pamphlet. December 21, married a widow, Mrs. Clairmont, mother of Jane "Claire" Clairmont.

1803   March 28, birth of son William. *The Life of Geoffrey Chaucer, the Early English Poet,* 2 volumes. Second edition, 4 volumes, 1804.

1805   *Fleetwood: or, The New Man of Feeling,* 3 volumes. Editions: London, 1805, 1832; New York, 1805; Paris, 1805. *Fables, Ancient and Modern,* by Edward Baldwin, Esq. (pseudonym) 2 volumes. *The Looking Glass: a True History of the Early Years of an Artist,* by Theophilus Marcliffe, Esq. (pseudonym). 1885 Facsimile Reprint.

1806   *The Pantheon: or Ancient History of the Gods of Greece and Rome,* by Edward Baldwin, Esq. (pseudonym). *The History of England,* by Edward Baldwin, Esq. (pseudonym).

1807   *Faulkener, a Tragedy in Prose,* played December 16 at Drury Lane Theatre; repeated several nights.

1809   *The History of Rome,* by Edward Baldwin, Esq. (pseudonym), for the Juvenile Library. *A New Guide to the English Tongue,* by Edward Baldwin, Esq. (pseudonym), for the Juvenile Library, Skinner Street, London. With the School Dictionary of W. F. Mylius. Second edition, 1815. *An Essay on Sepulchres,* published in both London and New York. *The Lives of Edward and John Philips, Nephews and Pupils of Milton,* Appendices: "Collections for the Life of Milton," by John Aubrey; "The Life of Milton," by Edward Philips. Editions: 1809, 1815.

1810   *Outlines of English Grammar: partly abridged from Mr. Hazlitt's New and Improved Grammar*, by Edward Baldwin, Esq. (pseudonym), for the Juvenile Library.

1811   *The History of Greece*, by Edward Baldwin, Esq. (pseudonym), for the Juvenile Library.

1814   July 28, Mary Godwin and Jane Clairmont joined Shelley, posted to Dover, crossed in open boat to Calais—pursued by Mrs. Godwin.

1816   October 11, Fanny Godwin, daughter of Captain Gilbert Imlay and Mary Wollstonecraft, committed suicide by laudanum, Mackworth Arms Inn, Swansea. November 9, Harriet Shelley drowned herself in the Serpentine, Kensington Gardens, London. Body found December 10. December 30, Percy Bysshe Shelley married Mary Godwin.

1817   *Mandeville, a Tale of the Seventeenth Century in England*, 3 volumes, Edinburgh. Editions: 2 volumes, New York, 1818; 4 volumes, Paris, 1819.

1818   *Letter of Advice to a Young American, on the Course of Studies most advantageous for him to pursue*, by M. J. Godwin, for the Juvenile Library.

1820   *Of Population: an Enquiry concerning the Power of Increase in the Numbers of Mankind; being an Answer to Mr. Malthus's Essay*. A 2-volume edition in Paris, 1821.

1822   Following Shelley's death in Italy, Mary Shelley returned to Godwin.

1824-
1828   *History of the Commonwealth of England, from its Commencement to the Restoration of Charles the Second*, 4 volumes.

1830   *Cloudesley*, 3 volumes.

1831   *Thoughts on Man, his Nature, Productions and Discoveries.*

1832   Death of son, William, of cholera, in the autumn. Son's novel, *Transfusion*, published after his death by Godwin, with Memoir.

1833   *Deloraine*, 3 volumes. In April, Lord Grey conferred on Godwin the sinecure post of Yeoman Usher of the Exchequer, with residence in New Palace Yard.

1834   *The Lives of the Necromancers: or, an Account of the Most Eminent Persons in Successive Ages, who have claimed for themselves, or to whom has been imputed by*

> *others, the Exercise of Magical Power.* Editions: London, 1834, 1876; New York, 1835, 1847.

1836   Died Thursday, April 7. Buried beside Mary Wollstonecraft, Old St. Pancras Churchyard. When churchyard cut by two railways, both bodies moved to Bournemouth Churchyard, beside Mary Shelley.

1873   *Essays,* published posthumously, in London, from unfinished series of vigorous essays on religious subjects, entitled *The Genius of Christianity Unveiled.*

William Godwin

CHAPTER 1

Introduction

"CHARLES, did you ever hear me preach?" Samuel Taylor Coleridge once asked Charles Lamb. "I never heard you do anything else," was his friend's reply.[1] The Romantic Era was full of preachers without pulpits, men who in an age of faith would have been eloquent and dedicated servants of the church, or in a later day equally dedicated servants of science; but, although deeply concerned with spiritual issues and evangelically apt to communicate their convictions, they were, in their age, disoriented from the Christian religion. William Godwin, born in 1756, came earlier than most of these secular clergymen, except William Blake; but Godwin's death in 1836 preceded by only one year the Victorian Era, which was replete with preachers who gave moral instruction everywhere but in church pulpits: Tennyson, Arnold, Carlyle, Ruskin, and Dickens—to name a few.

Godwin had better clerical credentials than most, for he had imbibed the stern creed of Calvinism with his mother's milk; had become a Sandemanian through his lessons, punctuated with salutary floggings by his tutor, Samuel Newton; and had been ordained to preach the Socinian Unitarian doctrine of Dr. Joseph Priestley,[2] a doctrine from which Godwin strayed into Theism, Deism, and eventually atheism. It would be a mistake, however, to think that "The Reverend William Godwin" occupied a slight or transitory portion of the life of the total man. There is no question but that he held each successive theological position with logical acumen and disputatious zeal.

In the last year of his academic life he engaged in a curious literary warfare with Mr. Richard Evans, a fellow student whom he described as "an excellent mathematician, and a man of very clear understanding." The subject was, of course, the existence of God. The intense epistolary interchange was engaged in with absolutely no audience but each other. Godwin wrote, with greater frankness than humility, "I took the negative side, in this instance, as always with great sincerity, hoping that my friend might enable me to remove the difficulties I apprehended. I did not fully see my ground as to this radical question, but I had little doubt that grant the being of a God, both the truth of Christianity, and the doctrines of Calvinism, followed by infallible inference." [3]

But, as a child of the Enlightenment, in whom theological dogma had softened to moral philosophy and Biblical revelation had been domesticated into the controlling power of Reason, Godwin tended to think first of man and mind and only latterly of God and the Church. And as a Romantic, he was bubbling with that intoxicating brew of Liberty, Nature, Iconoclasm, and Individualism. When we see him preaching to the neighbor children at the age of four,[4] participating in an epistolary theological contest with a school friend, turned away from one college because of the quite-justified suspicion that he was tainted with Sandemanianism, taking advantage of minor bickering in his last parish to escape to the city to mold morals with literature, Godwin is pursuing his métier through all the changes rung by the clashing bells of his time and place. Helvétius' *De l'Esprit* and Baron d'Holbach's militantly atheistic *Système de la Nature* might have rocked his faith in the relevance of the Christian Gospel to a revolutionary world; but they did not uproot the idea of the Kingdom of God—it simply became the Kingdom of Faith in the Perfectibility of Man. Men who could no longer be served by an outmoded religion might still be exalted by the vision of moral happiness.

The most useful mission in the world, Godwin thought, was to increase the welfare and happiness of mankind. If one were to compare the two institutions, the government and the church, the government clearly had more widespread, powerful effects. Thus the structure of politics is "the first and most important subject of human investigation." But Plato's *Republic*, Augustine's *Civitas Dei*, and Paine's *Rights of Man* failed to reach the root of the problem and were inadequate as blueprints for a higher order of political life. Godwin would base government on the nature and potentiality of men and thus ensure the production of the highest welfare and happiness. He would show men the truth about themselves, and that truth would set them free from the dominion of wrong political forms.[5] And so the road that led to London was not a way of cynicism and despair; it was the high road of the triumphant pilgrim who has replaced a moribund Messiah with a very live, controversial gospel. Godwin's calling was to provide the greatest happiness for men by the power, not of the tongue, but of the pen.

His early writings represent many genres. One novel of the year 1783 took all of ten days to write; another of the same year was accomplished in three weeks. There was that life of William Pitt which the author himself later described as "a very wretched attempt." There was the account of a seminary to be opened on Monday, August 4, 1783; the date passed and "Twelve Pupils" who were to be instructed "in the Greek, Latin, French, and English languages" never appeared, and so the "Seminary at Epsom" never materialized. He even dusted off six sermons and published them as *Sketches of History* (1784). But the real test of the author's personal powers and political influence still lay ahead, and Godwin knew it. After contributing desultorily to Sheridan's short-lived *Political Herald* and regularly to the liberal *New Annual Register,* edited by his former tutor at Hoxton, Dr. Andrew Kippis, Godwin severed his connections with political periodicals, and with incredible boldness he proposed to Robinson the bookseller that he could write a great political document, if only some money could be advanced for the period of the writing. Even more incredibly, Robinson agreed; and Godwin began, on July 10, 1791, to work on his magnum opus, *An Enquiry concerning the Principles of Political Justice, and Its Influence on General Virtue and Happiness.* After two years of intensive labor, Godwin published this work in January, 1793.

His boldness and Robinson's credulity were both well justified. The contemporary writer William Hazlitt testified that

No work in our time gave such a blow to the philosophical mind of the country as the celebrated *Enquiry concerning Political Justice.* Tom Paine was considered for the time as a Tom Fool to him; Paley an old woman; Edmund Burke a flashy sophist. Truth, moral truth, it was supposed had here taken up its abode; and these were the oracles of thought. "Throw aside your books on chemistry," said Wordsworth to a young man, a student in the Temple, "and read Godwin on Necessity." . . . Mr. Godwin indulged in extreme opinions, and carried with him all the most sanguine and fearless understandings of the time.[6]

An unknown author testifies: "In many places, perhaps some hundreds, in England and Scotland, copies were bought by subscription, and read aloud in meetings of the subscribers." [7]

Godwin was to add, with a wide range of effectiveness, plays, histories, essays, legal and sociological treatises, fables, textbooks, and debates to his list of endeavors. The novel which "clothed political theory in flesh," *Caleb Williams,* contributed to the development of the English and American novel as a literary force; and it is still to be found in college courses. And through poverty, calumny, heartbreak, Godwin "practiced what he preached"— albeit at times with modification, as in his marriage to Mary Wollstonecraft, before Mary Godwin's birth, and in his protest to the elopement of Mary Godwin and Percy Bysshe Shelley. It is fitting that the *Enquiry concerning Political Justice,* basic and preëminent, should be the subject of chapter two.

CHAPTER 2

Political Theory

"When Steelyard [William Godwin], the lawgiver, coming in stalk-
ing—with an act of parliament in his hand, said that it was a shameful
thing that acts of parliament should be in a free state, it had so en-
grossed his mind that he did not salute the company."
                    WILLIAM BLAKE, "An Island in the Moon."

*A*N *Enquiry concerning the Principles of Political Justice, and
     Its Influence on General Virtue and Happiness* is remarka-
ble for at least four qualities. First, it bristles with a multitude of
the incendiary comments that led Russell Noyes to call Godwin
"the most extreme of the revolutionary philosophers" [1] and James
Preu to characterize him as "one of the most extreme radicals of
all time." [2] Yet Godwin's comments are made modestly, in a
simple style which seems to assume that all men must acknowledge truths so self-evident. The deceptive innocence of utterance
gives a curious delayed-action explosiveness to the reading of his
pages. Godwin, in referring to his years at Hoxton, comments
with his characteristic arrogance: "I was remarked by my fellow-
collegians for the intrepidity of my opinions and the tranquil fearlessness of my temper." [3] Perhaps it is this unlikely combination of
tranquility and fearlessness that gives Godwin's pages both ambi-
guity and charm.

I *Incendiary Statement*

The statements which aroused the most clamor in his own era
and continued to sound ridiculous to later commentators include
these basic ideas: Truth is omnipotent. Vice is merely an error in
judgment. Man is perfectible. Government is the great obstacle to
human happiness. The operation of the law of necessity produces
inevitable progress. The private affections block universal benevolence. About these basic concepts Godwin wrote:

[23]

TRUTH IS OMNIPOTENT:

Sound reasoning and truth, when adequately communicated, must always be victorious over error. . . . Truth is omnipotent: The Vices and moral weakness of man are not invincible: Man is perfectible, or in other words susceptible of perpetual improvement (Book I, Chapter v).

If juries might at length cease to decide, and be contented to invite, if force might gradually be withdrawn and reason trusted alone, shall we not one day find, that juries themselves, and every other species of public institution, may be laid aside as unnecessary? (Book V, Chapter xxiv).

A virtuous and upright nation, would be scarcely more willing to mislead the enemy, by false intelligence, or treacherous ambuscade, than by the breach of their engagements, or by feigned demonstrations of friendship (Book V, Chapter xviii).

VICE IS MERELY AN ERROR IN JUDGMENT:

A man of certain intellectual habits, is fitted to be an assassin; a dagger of certain form, is fitted to be his instrument. . . . The man is propelled to act by necessary causes and irresistible motives, which, having once occurred, are likely to occur again. The dagger has no quality adapted to the contraction of habits, and though it have committed a thousand murders, is not more likely (unless so far as those murders, being known, may operate as a slight associated motive with the possessor) to commit murder again. Except in the articles here specified, the two cases are exactly parallel. The assassin cannot help the murder he commits, any more than the dagger (Book VII, Chapter i).

Every principle which can be brought home to the conviction of the mind will infallibly produce a correspondent effect upon the conduct (Book I, Chapter v).

Truth and virtue are competent to fight their own battles. They do not need to be nursed and patronized by the hand of power (Book VI, Chapter i).

A vicious conduct is always the result of narrow views (Book IV, Chapter v, Appendix).

A powerful understanding is inseparable from eminent virtue (Book IV, Chapter v, Appendix).

MAN IS PERFECTIBLE:

It is the characteristic of mind to be capable of improvement (Book VI, Chapter viii).

[24]

. . . marriage, as now understood, is a monopoly, and the worst of monopolies. . . . So long as I seek, by despotic and artificial means, to maintain my possession of a woman, I am guilty of the most odious selfishness. . . . All . . . arguments are calculated to determine our judgment in favour of marriage as a salutary and respectable institution, but not of that species of marriage, in which there is no room for repentance, and to which liberty and hope are equally strangers. . . . Certainly no ties ought to be imposed upon either party preventing them from quitting the attachment, whenever their judgment directs them to quit it. With respect to such infidelities as are compatible with an intention to adhere to it, the point of principal importance is a determination to have recourse to no species of disguise (Book VIII, Chapter viii, Appendix).

GOVERNMENT IS THE GREAT OBSTACLE TO HUMAN HAPPINESS:

Political enquiry had long held a considerable place in the writer's attention. It is now twelve years since he became satisfied, that monarchy was a species of government essentially corrupt (Preface, p. ix, First Edition).

But there are [also] certain disadvantages, that may seem the necessary result of democratical equality. In political society, it is reasonable to suppose, that the wise will be outnumbered by the unwise; and it will be inferred "that the welfare of the whole, will therefore be at the mercy of ignorance and folly." . . . The turbulent and crafty demagogue, will often possess greater advantages for inveigling their judgment, than the man who, with pure intentions, may possess a less brilliant talent (Book V, Chapter xiv).

Government can have no more than two legitimate purposes, the suppression of injustice against individuals within the community, and the common defence against external invasion (Book V, Chapter xxii).

It is in vain that we endeavour to counteract the laws of nature and necessity. A multitude of men, after all our ingenuity, will still remain a multitude of men. Nothing can intellectually unite them short of equal capacity and identical perception. So long as the varieties of mind shall remain, the force of society can no otherwise be concentrated than by one man, for a shorter or a longer term, taking the lead of the rest, and employing their force, whether material, or dependent on the weight of their character, in a mechanical manner, just as he would employ the force of a tool or a machine. All government corresponds, in a certain degree, to what the Greeks denominated a tyranny (Book V, Chapter xxiii).

Too much stress has undoubtedly been laid upon the idea, as of a

[25]

grand and magnificent spectacle, of a nation deciding for itself upon some great public principle, and of the highest magistracy yielding its claims when the general voice has pronounced. The value of the whole must at last depend upon the quality of their decision. Truth cannot be made more true by the number of its votaries (Book III, Chapter iv).

PRIVATE AFFECTIONS BLOCK UNIVERSAL BENEVOLENCE:

A man is of more worth than a beast; because, being possessed of higher faculties, he is capable of a more refined and genuine happiness. In the same manner the illustrious archbishop of Cambray was of more worth than his valet, and there are few of us that would hesitate to pronounce, if his palace were in flames, and the life of only one of them could be preserved, which of the two ought to be preferred. . . . Suppose I had been myself the valet; I ought to have chosen to die, rather than Fénelon should have died. The life of Fénelon was really preferable to that of the valet. . . . Suppose the valet had been my brother, my father or my benefactor. This would not alter the truth of the proposition. The life of Fénelon would still be more valuable than that of the valet; and justice, pure, and unadulterated justice, would still have preferred that which was most valuable. Justice would have taught me to save the life of Fénelon at the expense of the other. What magic is there in the pronoun "my," that should justify us in overturning the decisions of impartial truth? My brother or my father may be a fool or a profligate, malicious, lying or dishonest. If they be, of what consequence is it that they are mine? (Book II, Chapter ii).

II *Complex Unity of Structure*

Even in modern times these sample statements from Godwin's writing could seem incendiary. Only careful reading will reveal the second of the remarkable qualities of the *Enquiry concerning Political Justice and Its influence on Morals and Happiness*—the complex unity of its structure stated in an aphoristic style, somewhat in the manner of Spinoza. As the full title suggests, the political structure is discussed in terms of justice; hence its value is considered less in terms of security and power, than in those of virtue and happiness. For one of Godwin's cast of mind, a political philosophy presupposes a moral philosophy, and a moral philosophy must rest upon metaphysical and psychological presuppositions. Thus the book is political and historical; psychological and philosophical; and, above all, moralistic. An analysis of the total structure of thought in *Political Justice* gives a frame of reference for the isolated ideas which have already been presented.

Book I considers the capacity of man in his social functions. It begins with a survey of the history of political society and proceeds to an examination of the spirit of political institutions. It discovers that robbery and fraud, two great vices of society, originate in extreme poverty and in the ostentation and tyranny of the rich. But they become permanent parts of social life because of legislation, the administration of the law, and the manner in which property is distributed.

Just as robbery and fraud originate and are encouraged from outside a man, men's characters originate in their external circumstances. There are no innate characteristics present at birth, no instinctive actions. Of course, there is a minor effect of heredity, peculiarity of structure, and some prenatal impressions. But these are exceedingly unimportant by comparison with the bulk of a man's total life-experience. Men receive character, personality, and conviction from the external world of sensation. Then from this received character arise the voluntary actions of men. Men are especially sensitive to receive truth, which, when adequately presented, is always victorious over falsehood. Vice is simple error of judgment—an error which will be perceived and corrected; for man is perpetually capable of and disposed to improvement. By the analogy of human invention, just as any machine can always be improved, just so is man susceptible to perpetual improvement.

Book II of *Political Justice* deals with the principles of human society. Society—the gathering of men into community—expresses men's desires and can be a source of great blessing. Government, on the other hand, arises out of men's wickedness and their needs for restraint and authority; and it is, at best, a necessary evil; at worst, a curse. Government never has the right or power to decide what is the social good; it must simply reflect the moral convictions of its members. Justice may be defined as the combination of self-love and civic usefulness that produces genuine benevolence. Thus, in politics, a man's individuality should be protected, and yet the spheres of individualism must be kept from overlapping. Men are physically and morally equal. They have great capacity for both personal virtue and societal duty. A man may occasionally err in benevolence, be confused by the mutability of belief, or become lost in the complexity of motive. But it never becomes his duty to do wrong, even if a state were to order him to do so.

If government has no rights, does man? He has no active rights; that is, the right to do as he likes in all cases. But he does have passive rights, to expect the forbearance or assistance of other men. His central right, the right of private judgment, is the foundation of all virtue. Although political institutions are not generally efficacious in exciting virtue or in informing the judgment, they often attempt to invade the realm of private conscience and, by punishment, to enforce their own wrong principles.

Books I and II consider man as a social animal and deduce the principles of his relationships with others. Book III delineates the principles of government. Three hypotheses of the historical origin of government are explored and rejected: superior strength, divine edict, social contract. The true foundation of government is in the common deliberations of the governed. Therefore, reverence or fear are not owed to governments, which are themselves derivative. Government can never claim more than a man's rational obedience.

What is the relationship of a man's personal opinions (convictions) to the established laws and traditions of his government? Book IV reminds each man that he has the right of resistance to specific edicts of his government whether he is in the majority, the minority, or stands as a single individual. A citizen has no duty to the constitution of his country, which may be a good constitution or a bad one, but which certainly ought to change continually. But revolutionary measures, during their operation, are inimical to independence and to intellectual enquiry. They are bloody, crude, and premature in their immediate effects and uncertain in their outcome. Conviction of the understanding of the individual by education and persuasion are the only adequate means of abolishing political abuse. Yet established abuses may be so deeprooted and held with such a frenzy of unreason, that revolutionary violence may have to be resorted to. Political associations, which are established for the good purpose of improving government, may in their own turn become attended by the party spirit, declamation, cabal, contentious disputes, restlessness, and tumult.

Truth has the power to improve political institutions, and constantly tends to do so. This kind of useful truth is scientific, the result of careful, impartial investigation. Fortunately, in the mass of individual opinion men resemble each other in more ways than they differ, and they all have the common need to be made free, virtuous, and wise. Thus the duties we owe to each other have a common area of agreement, a core of truth.

Eminent virtue and a cultivated mind always go together. Yet to imagine that the will is free is to harbor an injurious error. The doctrine of necessity leads us to the greatest efforts to influence for good the formation of men's characters. It moves out of the area of caprice and accident (free will), into the area of sure causation (necessity). The mind operates within the framework of sensational causality, using clusters of sensations for complex ideas. The mind is always thinking, with the utmost rapid succession of ideas. It is thought which produces animal motion.

It is benevolence, not self-love, that is most compatible with the production of virtue. A voluntary act of kindness excites pleasure in the bestower. As the single voluntary act is repeated, it tends to become habit, and habit finally becomes reflex action. Thus benevolence, rather than self-love, becomes the root of relationship with others. Good is pleasure and evil is pain. But pleasure includes giving pleasure to others and the contemplation of the enjoyments of other men. Pleasure may come from the common life of the farmer or the artisan, from the enjoyment of great wealth, from the application of the most cultivated taste; but, above all, it comes from the practice of benevolence.

Book V considers the powers of the legislative and executive branches of government. It comes to the conclusion that government is an evil which usurps private judgment and individual conscience. It may be a necessary evil for the present, but it ought constantly to shrink away as the human mind develops. This expectation is, for Godwin, a kind of millennial hope. He exults, along with all men of good will, in the anticipation of a golden age of self-controlled individualism; then political jurisdiction will shrivel to nothing—"that brute engine, which has been the only perennial cause of the vices of mankind, and which . . . has mischiefs of various sorts incorporated with its substance, and no otherwise removable than by its utter annihilation!" (Book V, Chapter xxiv).

One of the outstanding examples of these "incorporated mischiefs" is found in the institution of monarchy. The education of a prince treats him as superior to other men; and it makes him childish, capricious, and in love with power. Monarchy is based on the imposture that to any one man is due the reverence and adulation of other men because of his birth or station. Monarchy, whether extreme or limited, always produces venality and corruption in the state. It rules by flattery, bribery, caprice, and display; and, worst of all, it produces these same characteristics in all the descending ranks of its hierarchies. But in considering monarchy the outstanding example of those "incorporated mischiefs" which require not the reformation but annihilation, we must not forget that republics and democracies also have their inherent evils. For example, in democracy it is almost impossible, if the democracy be real and pure, to avoid the ascendancy of the ignorant and the rule of the demagogue who sways them.

Government has been prolific in the production of wars. Yet just as government can have only two legitimate purposes: the suppression of injustice against individuals within the community, and the common defence against external invasion, there can be only two just causes of war: defence of our own liberty, and the defence of the liberty of others.

If the individual opinions of men are the source of political institutions, how should political institutions attempt to control those opinions? Book VI states that governments ought not to establish a particular religion, or make any attempt to suppress differing opinions in religion and government. Tests, oaths, and libel laws all hamper the development of a healthy sincerity in public life. Government certainly ought not to supervise national education lest it attempt to educate in accordance with its own established policies. For a government to give or the individual to receive pensions or salaries is to establish a pressure within those individuals against the expression of private opinions and for the expression of recognized and accepted public opinion.

Book VII follows the discussion of the relation between individual opinion and political dogma with its application to crime and punishment. Criminal punishment may be enacted only for the necessary restraint of one who might be a danger to the community, and for the reformation of the criminal. The criminal is the result of the influences society has brought to bear upon him. Ought the source of his crime punish him for the commission of that crime? The lawbreaker ought to be dealt with through persuasion and the self-evident power of truth, rather than by punishment, restraint, or preconceived ideas of suitable reformation.

Book VIII is concerned with the ownership of property and recognizes that most of law and government arise out of the desire to protect ownership. It states as its formula of possession that every man has a right to that which, having been awarded to him as an exclusive possession, produces a greater sum of civic benefit or public pleasure than could have arisen from its being otherwise appropriated. The good things of this world are a common stock, upon which one man has as valid a title as another to draw for what he needs. Each man has a sphere, the limit and termination of which is marked out by the equal sphere of his neighbor. Inherited and accumulated property ought to be dispersed as rapidly as possible without harming the public welfare.

The current laws of the church and the state on so sacred and individual a theme as love and marriage tend to treat them as forms of ownership. Cooperation, cohabitation, and marriage must always be secondary to the prime importance of the freedom of the individual. Thus cooperation must maintain moral independence, and marriage must never become an involuntary bondage.

The work closes with a secular apocalyptic vision of the future success of the principle of free equality:

There will be no war, no crimes, no administration of justice, as it is called, and government. Beside this, there will be neither disease, anguish, melancholy, nor resentment. Every man will seek, with ineffable ardour, the good of all. Mind will be active and eager, yet never disappointed. Men will see the progressive advancement of virtue and good, and feel that, if things occasionally happen contrary to their hopes, the miscarriage itself was a necessary part of that progress. They will know, that they are members of the chain, that each has his several utility, and they will not feel indifferent to that utility. They will be eager to enquire into the good that already exists, the means by which it was produced, and the greater good that is yet in store. They will never want motives for exertion; for that benefit which a man thoroughly understands and earnestly loves, he cannot refrain from endeavouring to promote (Book VIII, Chapter ix, Appendix).

Once the incendiary statements, which gained for Godwin the reputation of being the most radical mind ever produced in England, are set in their appropriate places in the structure of the whole thought, they seem not only less strange, but even inevitable. There is a certain glacial logic in which these hot aphorisms burn with the brightness of ice fragments.

Godwin maintains the first of his challenging maxims—truth is omnipotent—not because it is a Platonic idea, nor because it bears a particular religious sanction, but because its omnipotence is the necessary corollary of the persuasibility of human reason. A man need not be forced, cajoled, fooled or restrained into doing the thing he ought to do. His mind is perfectly capable of receiving truth, recognizing that it is truth by its very superior persuasiveness, and then acting upon that truth by the inner cohesion that exists between opinion and action. Truth's omnipotence does not rest on its eternality or innateness, but upon its persuasiveness to a persuadable mind.

Godwin's faith in persuasion is not quite so extreme as it seems. All the world's great teachers seem to have felt there was a particular power in the spoken word to open the closed mind to the homing good. "And ye shall know the truth and the truth shall make you free" (John 8:32). "One word, happily interposed, reaching to his inmost soul, may take away a heart of stone and introduce a heart of flesh," Godwin says in *Thoughts on Man;* and again, "sudden and irresistible conviction is chiefly the offspring of living speech." J. Middleton Murry comments that it was probably "due to his painstaking endeavor to achieve this miracle that he, although a poor talker, became so enamoured of 'colloquial discussion' and the 'collision of minds.'" [4] William Blake, Godwin's contemporary, offered the same tribute to truth, in strikingly similar language. "Truth," said Blake, "cannot be uttered so as to be understood and not be believed." [5] Yet all that Godwin meant by "positive institutions" is symbolized in Blake's arch-enemy Urizen. So reason was for Blake, the devil; and for Godwin, the savior.

They said the same things with precisely the opposite meanings. (Perhaps their only real unity was that they both loved Mary Wollstonecraft, who loved William Godwin.)[6]

It is this irresistible power of truth which forces the logical conclusion of Godwin's second contention: vice is merely an error in judgment. Vice occurs from the lack of a cultivated mind. Vice cannot spring from a doctrine of original sin because this would be a kind of innate idea, a warping of the individual at birth. Instead, the mind coolly assesses all the sensations that are its due, and from the total determines which are true and good. Even a man of great natural talents for discernment may occasionally make a mistake in judgment and a consequent error in morality, for the conduct always arises out of the opinions. But, when he is exposed to truth and his mind has grown in its capacity for discernment, he will recognize his error and rectify it in suitable conduct.

Reason, for Godwin, seems to be a kind of Spinozistic *scientia intuitiva*. As F. E. L. Priestley points out, "reason not only judges the rightness of an action or the desirability of an end, but irresistibly urges toward that action or towards the pursuit of that end: it is not merely cognitive, but has an appetitive aspect." [7] Thus morality is reduced to recognition on the plane of reason, just as on the plane of conduct it is reduced to the predictive summing-up of probable consequences. Reason, then, gives us the power of "going out of ourselves," of becoming "impartial spectators of the system of which we are a part" (Book IV, Chapter x).

Godwin's mind has an interesting psychological pattern which might be called the *reductio* not *absurdum* but *simplicitatem*. Eschewing all the high-flown rhetoric about crime and punishment, all the harrowing accounts that have been emotionally written, he slips easily, quietly, conversationally into the tone of one propounding matters of fact with which there can be, of course, no argument. And so he goes about calmly exposing kings, revealing the impostures of monarchy, and demolishing the sanctity of marriage vows in a single paragraph.[8] He regretfully admits that it may occasionally be necessary to resist murderers by force, but it is folly to attempt to punish them. Force is not an argument, and accusation of a criminal becomes the attempt to spank a knife.

Law, in its next-to-final step toward dissolution, should be a jury which invites the accused to meet with it and simply exposes him to a recital of his self-evident errors and duties. If individuality is the central sanctity of mortal life, then no man, even one accused of crime, ought to be coerced, forced, or punished. Indeed, such invasions of his personal rights are unnecessary because reason, truth's viceroy in the human personality, will convince him of his error; truth will have its sure power of persuasion. Thus what the block, gibbet, scaffold, and noose were unable to do, can be accomplished pleasantly and simply by a group of men who share—without vehemence or insistence—their own understanding of the truth.

To punish the murderer is as absurd as chastising the knife with which he did the deed, because a man is simply the product of all the sensations that have played upon his receptive mind. He did not choose those sensations; he was essentially passive in his relation to them. He did not inherit a tendency toward murder, nor was it an incipient innate idea, for he was born almost totally devoid of specific tendency. Indeed, to say that he murdered because of original sin or natural depravity or biological determinism would equally absolve the murderer from personal responsibility for his crime, and therefore from punishment for his crime. In the crime, both were instruments, rather than instrument and agent: the knife in the hand of the murderer, the murderer in the hands of the social order that formed him.

This social responsibility for the individual's personality is the key to Godwin's third principle—the perfectibility of man. Man is perfectible, continually capable of improvement, simply because his nature is malleable. If his character had been marred by original sin or by the stain of the natural man, he would require some major and drastic reformation before he could begin the road to perfection. But he can grow perpetually because he comes into the world naked of presuppositions and then becomes enriched by the sum total of all the impressions that play upon his impressionable form. There is no limit to the growth potential of one who is being bombarded, lifelong, with the stuff of growth.

When the theory that character is molded by external forces beyond the control of the individual is held by an optimistic philosopher like William Godwin, it comes very close to the doctrine of the innate goodness of the natural and primitive man held by

Jean Jacques Rousseau. The absence of evil from man at birth and his propensity toward reason, truth, and perpetual improvement suggest that, for Godwin, man was more like Tom Jones's "good nature" than like Locke's *tabula rasa*. And in stating that vice is error and society is responsible for existent evil, Godwin throws wide the door to literary sentimentalism—every erring creature, every victim of society is worthy of persuasion and, perhaps, pity.[9] But Godwin could inflict his tolerance like a wound. When John Thelwall was in the Tower of London awaiting trial for high treason, Godwin took him severely to task for his resentment against those who seemed to be actively persecuting him: "How senseless and idiot-like it is to be angry with what we know to be mere passive instrument, moved according to certain regular principles and in no degree responsible for its operations." [10] The reminder may not have been particularly comforting or palatable to the prisoner, but the remark was entirely consistent with Godwin's philosophy. It was doubtless this stern consistency that earned Hazlitt's paradox: "Mr. Godwin possesses a high degree of philosophical candour, and studiously paid the homage of his pen and person to Mr. Malthus, Sir James Mackintosh, and Dr. Parr, for their unsparing attacks on him; but woe to any poor devil who had the hardihood to defend him against them!" [11]

It is interesting to note that no matter how dark Godwin's estimate of the present state of man, his estimate of man's basic nature and potentialities is bright with hope. In a letter to his patron, Thomas Wedgwood, Godwin judges Dr. Samuel Johnson unfavorably because of his dark view of human nature: "Allow me to recommend to you a very cautious admission of the moral apothegms of Doctor Johnson. He had an unprecedented tendency to dwell on the dark and unamiable side of our nature. I love him less than most other men of equal talents and intentions, because I cannot reasonably doubt that when he drew so odious a picture of man he found some of the traits in his own bosom." [12]

William Godwin's doctrine of the perfectibility of man was related to the many vigorous reform movements which sprang up in England under the liberating influence of the French Revolution. In the British parliament, Charles James Fox, the leader of the Whig party, hailed the fall of the Bastille as the greatest and best event in human history; Thomas Paine issued his *Rights of Man* in reply to Edmund Burke's reactionary *Reflections on the Revolution in France.* Many reform societies were organized or revitalized, ranging from the aristocratic and conservative "Friends of the People" to the proletarian and radical "London Corresponding Society."

Just as in the twentieth century the "Technocracy" movement grew out of technological achievement, in the eighteenth century men hoped to discover in the realms of psychology, ethics, morality, and sociology, laws just as certain and universal as the Newtonian laws of physical structure. If such laws could be discovered —and men were enthusiastically certain they could—all of human society might take a great step forward and experience a moral transformation the equal of the material transformations that were so radically altering the lives of men everywhere.

Optimistically, Godwin believed that moral transformation need not precede the removal of governing institutions; rather, its arrival would be hastened by the dissolution of these institutions. One such restriction—marriage—he considered the worst of all monopolies because it involved accumulated property in which a sacred individual was the property. No person ought to "own" or be "owned." No individual should be in subjection to another individual. No perfectible man, or woman, continually changing, ought to be bound by promises which reflected previous feelings no longer appropriate in a present relationship. Indeed, in any relationship there is inherent this problem of the maintenance of personal conviction and the practice of general benevolence. During Jesus' Galilean ministry, while He was preaching to a great crowd, a message was brought that His mother and brethren were out at the edge of the throng, waiting to speak to Him. But to this perfectly normal domestic request, Jesus replied, "Who is my mother? and who are my brethren?" And stretching out His hands toward his disciples, He said, "Behold, my mother and my brethren! For whosoever shall do the will of my Father which is in heaven, he is my brother, and sister, and mother" (Matthew 12:46-50).

It is important to note that Godwin's strictures on marriage related to both liberty and growth. In every relationship, a person ought to remain free to continue or sever the bond. This is an expression of Godwin's passionate conviction concerning human freedom. But he also has in mind the problems of growth. A growing personality must not be bound by the promises of the past. The old self must not cripple and confine the new, emerging self if there is to be any hope for the development of the body politic. But his protest against bondage was considered a campaign for the abolishment of marriage; his support of the claims of growth was construed as a plea for sexual license.[13]

The absolutism of Godwin's thinking made him cast a jaundiced eye on all groups that submerged individualism. Does it sound ridiculous to quibble about being asked to play in an orchestra when all of one's personal idiosyncrasies cry out for a solo? Nevertheless this is a worthy analogy and illustration of the problem of necessary subordination to the total design along with the requirement that each man express himself. Perhaps even orchestras will some day seem an unnecessary tyranny, and each man will play alone the melody that expresses him and him alone. To Godwin ". . . everything understood by the term co-operation is in some senses an evil." [14] Acting in plays presents an even greater difficulty, the problem of the manifest breach of the law of sincerity. How can a man with decorum adopt the imposture of seeming to be another man? And if a man's character is pelted upon him by circumstance, how can he attempt to play another character as if personality came from the inside out?

A second great obstacle to man's individual growth is government. It is the great obstacle to human happiness simply because it will not die. As a necessary instrument to keep the individual "spheres of discretion" from collision, it ought to atrophy as its use becomes less obligatory. Instead, it is the nature of government to increase and spread, to take to itself all the prerogatives of self and society, and even to reach out in aggrandizement upon the territory of other governments. The problem is not with the form of government, be it monarchy or democracy; it is with the very nature of government itself. What began by being a small necessary evil has become instead the colossal center of infection and dislocation for all rational social life.

At the outset of his task, Godwin had naturally assumed that good government was a powerful agency for promoting human welfare and only bad government was an enemy of human happiness and growth. But as he worked, the facts of the past sharpened his perceptions and forced a historical judgment upon him. Government, which was supposed to protect life and property, had instead plunged nation after nation into wars in which thousands of persons lost their lives and vast amounts of property were destroyed.

Oliver Goldsmith, in *The Vicar of Wakefield* (Chapter xix), defended monarchy as the protector of the poor against the aristocracy. Henry Fielding, in *Tom Jones* (Book XII, Chapter xii), maintained "it is the best and most desirable of all forms under a good and virtuous prince." But Godwin's reading in Jonathan Swift and in the Latin historians had already convinced him of the corruption inherent in a monarchial system of government. And when he turned to the Fourth Book of *Gulliver's Travels*, with its description of the society of the Houyhnhnms, he noted that they were strangers to poverty and great accumulations of wealth; they had no wars and no vices. Perhaps this blessed condition was not the reason for little need of government or law, but the result of their absence. If Swift could imagine such an anarchistic utopia among horses, was it out of the question that men might someday achieve a society of totally free men? [15]

Rousseau considered government as essential to human existence. Its origin was veiled in savagery, tyranny, and men's necessary adjustments to the development of social relationships. If, in its original advent, it was a necessary evil, now let it become a moral necessity. J. Middleton Murry writes that "society might become the means to a new kind of human liberty—these positions were strictly incomprehensible to Godwin. The notion that men might need to be 'forced to be free' was worse than a paradox to him; it was a blasphemy . . . His thought was, in essence, independent, millennial and anarchical." [16]

Shelley's Prometheus expressed the central peculiarity of Godwin's attitude toward government. It is not so much against the force of government as against any force that Godwin protests. Force exerted upon reason produces only stubborn rebellion or supine acquiescence. Force exerted upon self-love to produce universal benevolence could at most produce conformity and dull uniformity. Governmental repression and political association for reform have this in common: they are both forms of organization which may further their ends by force. The basic unit, the final goal, must always be the individual, not the nation (Book II, Chapter iii). One of the serious indictments of government is that it creates a falsehood—the nation—or creates prejudice in honor of a particular social class. Through these unreal points of view we glimpse the world, and men look small and states look great, whereas just the reverse is true. Thus governments distort man's understanding of his own world.

When man's understanding is enlightened, he will accept the fifth of Godwin's revolutionary maxims: the private affections block universal benevolence. Charles Lamb called Godwin the "counsel for Archbishop Fénelon versus my own mother, in the famous fire cause." [17] Even Godwin must have recognized that his illustration was a bit strong, and he watered it down to "father or brother" in the second and third editions. With the imperturbable logic that shocked some of his contemporaries and amused others, Godwin asserted that the principle of public utility required the rescue of a great man rather than a close relative.[18] The Abbé Fénelon, rather than mother, sister, brother, father, or valet, ought to be rescued from the burning building because at some point men must tear themselves away from private interest and self-love and express that most exalted of characteristics, general benevolence. Here Godwin makes a significant break with the "selfish" theories of the English utilitarian philosophers. They had insisted that the highest, indeed, the only virtue of man is to obtain his own pleasure. Even "enlightened self-interest," while it made a passing bow toward the mob, paused in actual adoration only before the self. Godwin breaks this nexus by the power of pleasure derived from doing and witnessing the good of others. Thus, the "greatest good of the greatest number" develops a base which is truly social rather than basically personal and therefore selfish.

The benevolent action may be performed, in the first instance, simply to escape the disagreeable sight of another's distress. But, through the operation of habit, benevolence will be done for the pleasurable sensation the action itself imparts. Reason, in the meantime, acts as ambassador for a genuine altruism by reminding the individual of all the good social reasons for considering the best interests of one's neighbor. As a political program, such an expectation may border on absurdity, but is its faith in reason any greater than Plato's faith in the ideal in *The Republic,* or Rousseau's appeal to sentiment in the *Social Contract?*

All "private affections" are bad not in themselves, but in the sense that they imply partiality and hence injustice. Gratitude itself can become a vice, when it tends toward unfair favoring of a benefactor. Family feeling, delightful though it may be within the circle of inclusion, is, without the circle, a means of exclusion. If private affection can lead to social affection, and concern for *meum* become equal concern for *teum,* this would be the proper functioning of private love. But if family, marriage, filial relationship, or any or all existing social ties should be an obstacle in the way of the coming of universal benevolence, they should go. Leslie Stephen remarks that "Nobody . . . ever made so clean a sweep of all existing social ties, but he always preserves the calm and benevolent tone of a preacher, drawing obvious morals from the Sermon on the Mount, though the Christian creed is among the doctrines too absurd to require explicit confutation." [19]

Godwin stood with his predecessors whose faith in perfectibility was rooted in the psychological theory that all ideas are the sum of sensations, and not in any way fixed or innate. But when he combined with this commonly accepted view the dual insistences that vice arises out of intellectual error and that such error, once recognized, might easily be corrected, Body and Passion pale to insubstantial shadows, easily subdued by giant Reason. It is out of this coupling of current psychology and philosophical optimism that Godwin derived his exaggerated idea of the dominion of reason and benevolence over conduct, and his inadequate recognition of those deep and primitive forces in human nature that reject the sovereignty of mind. For Godwin, "All that we observe that is best and most excellent in the intellectual world, is man." [20]

In a wise and witty passage, William Hazlitt recognized Godwin's inadequate estimate of the selfishness of men, but also pointed out that such an error was on the side of the angels:

The fault, then, of Mr. Godwin's philosophy, in a word, was too much ambition—"by that sin fell the angels." He conceived too nobly of his fellows (the most unpardonable crime against them, for there is nothing that annoys our self-love so much as being complimented on imaginary achievements, to which we are wholly unequal)—he raised the standard of morality above the reach of humanity, and by directing virtue to the most airy and romantic heights, made her path dangerous, solitary, and impracticable. The author of the *Political Justice* took abstract reason for the rule of conduct, and abstract good for its end. . . . Mr. Godwin gives no quarter to the amiable weaknesses of our nature, nor does he stoop to avail himself of the supplementary aids of an imperfect virtue. Gratitude, promises, friendship, family affection give way, not that they may be merged in the opposite vices or in want of principle; but that the void may be filled up by the disinterested love of good, and the dictates of inflexible justice, which is "the law of laws, and sovereign of sovereigns." . . . Mr. Godwin's theory, and that of more approved reasoners, differ only in this, that what are with them the exceptions, the extreme cases he makes the everyday rule. No one denies that on great occasions, in moments of fearful excitement, or when a mighty object is at stake, the lesser and merely instrumental points of duty are to be sacrificed without remorse at the shrine of patriotism, of honour, and of conscience. But the disciple of the *New School* (no wonder it found so many impugners, even in its own bosom!) is to be always the hero of duty. . . . If it be said that this scheme is chimerical and impracticable on ordinary occasions, and to the generality of mankind, well and good; but those who accuse the author of having trampled on the common feelings and prejudices of mankind in wantonness or insult, or without wishing to substitute something better (and only unattainable, because it is better) in their stead, accuse him wrongfully. We may not be able to launch the bark of our affections on the ocean-tide of humanity, we may be forced to paddle along its shores, or shelter in its creeks and rivulets; but we have no right to reproach the bold and adventurous pilot, who dared us to tempt the uncertain abyss, with our own want of courage or of skill, or with the jealousies and impatience, which deter us from undertaking, or might prevent us from accomplishing the voyage! [21]

III *Derivation of Thought*

Of the four significant qualities of the *Enquiry concerning Political Justice,* the first was the incendiary comments presented in a sincerely innocent manner. The second quality was the glacial logic of the total structure, once the author's original premises were granted. The third remarkable feature is the wide-ranging field from which its thought is derived. The pastor of a dissenting congregation, Godwin made religious nonconformity extend into the field of political radicalism, like that of his celebrated contemporaries, Dr. Joseph Priestley and Dr. Richard Price. His Calvinistic doctrine of predestination undoubtedly prepared him for acceptance of a theory of "philosophical necessity." John Calvin and Jonathan Edwards were exchanged for the intellectual comradeship of the French Encyclopedists, the English utilitarians, and Jean Jacques Rousseau, although both the theological and the philosophical relationships were within definite limits and with distinct reservations. The pulpit was exchanged for the printed page, but the moral fervor of the preacher remained the same.[22] The much-derided doctrine of the "perfectibility of man" may be a simple extension on the secular plane of the faith of the saints in the possibility of spiritual and moral regeneration.[23]

Godwin's grandfather and father had both been Independent ministers. He himself was rejected from entrance to the Dissenting College at Homerton because of a well-founded suspicion that he was tainted with the heresy of Sandemanianism. Godwin described Sandeman as one "who, after Calvin had damned ninety-nine in a hundred of mankind, had contrived a scheme for damning ninety-nine in a hundred of the followers of Calvin." [24] As one of the "primitive sects" of Protestantism, the Sandemanians, who were to number Michael Faraday among their members in the next generation, attempted to live the faith of the New Testament in the world of today. They accepted the communism of the Acts of the Apostles as normative for modern Christians. All members were required to hold their personal property at the disposal of the Church for the relief of the poor among the fellowship. As members of an embattled little sect of Independents, they considered a state church unbiblical, and opposed with all their power any attempt of secular government to compel religious conformity. The certainty of "election" was a rarity among the Calvinists, because of the caprice of a sovereign God. But the Sandemanians were concerned with the rarity of genuinely Christian behavior in a supposedly Christian world.[25]

As a Protestant, Godwin had the long tradition of Puritan theology behind him. As a Sandemanian, he represented the even older anarchism, communism, and noninstitutionality of the church of the New Testament.²⁶ William Hazlitt immediately recognized and pointed out that

The *Enquiry concerning Political Justice* is a metaphysical and logical commentary on some of the most beautiful and striking texts of Scripture. Mr. Godwin is a mixture of the Stoic and of the Christian philosopher. To break the force of the vulgar objections and outcry that have been raised against the Modern Philosophy, as if it were a new and monstrous birth in morals, it may be worth noticing, that volumes of sermons have been written to excuse the founder of Christianity for not including friendship and private affection among its golden rules, but rather excluding them. Moreover, the answer to the question— "Who is thy neighbour?" added to the divine precept, "Thou shalt love thy neighbour as thyself," is the same as the exploded pages of our author—"he to whom we can do most good." . . . Our ardent and dauntless reformer followed out the moral of the parable of the Good Samaritan into its most rigid and repulsive consequences with pen of steel, and let fall his "trenchant-blade" on every vulnerable point of human infirmity, but there is a want in his system of the mild and persuasive tone of the Gospel, where "all is conscience and tender heart." Man was indeed screwed up, by mood and figure, into a logical machine, that was to forward the public good with the utmost punctuality and effect, and it might go very well on smooth ground and under favorable circumstances. . . . It was to be feared that the proud Temple of Reason, which at a distance and in stately supposition shone like the palaces of the New Jerusalem, might (when placed on actual ground) be broken up into the sordid styes of sensuality, and the petty huckster's shops of self-interest! ²⁷

A second source of *Political Justice* is the epistemology of John Locke. Godwin derived from Helvétius the Lockean idea that man is the product of his education, the sum total of all the influences that play upon him from his very birth. Locke's psychology, as developed through the associationalist theories of John Gay and David Hartley in England and through Abbé de Condillac in France, stated that sensations, linked together by association, are the stuff of which the mind of man is made. At its birth, the mind is a *tabula rasa,* said Locke. The environment writes upon the "blank tablet" and establishes its character. Far from being a pessimistic determinism, the hopefulness of the theory lay in the possibility that alteration of the environment would necessarily produce alteration in the character. If these environmental changes were for the good, the resulting changes in character and personality would be in the direction of improvement. Thus human character is divorced from the tyranny of innate ideas, the premature damnation of the doctrine of original sin, and the caprice of free will. Instead, human conduct is governed by the principle of necessity. The manipulation of environment must have an immediate and predictable effect on opinion, which, in turn, determines conduct. Virtuous conduct, in turn, is determined by the criterion of utility: does it produce the greatest happiness for the greatest number? [28]

All of these epistemological positions were clearly derivative from contemporary sources, but it was the creative genius of Godwin which bound them together with Christian ethics and humanistic optimism. D. H. Monro called Godwinism "the offspring of French intelligence and the English nonconformist conscience." [29] Hazlitt referred to Godwin as a "metaphysician engrafted on the Dissenting Minister." [30]

In the Preface to *Political Justice*, Godwin mentioned specifically his indebtedness to two French *philosophes*, Helvétius and d'Holbach. Thus it was through his mind that the French Encyclopaedic Revolt made its entry into the English scene. Although he broke with Helvétius on the "selfish" theory and with Rousseau on the "social contract" and the innate goodness of the natural man, the distillation of French thought in his treatise left a residue of conviction and faith for the English reader. [31]

Godwin acknowledges other influences when he says, in the Preface to the first edition. "It is now twelve years since [the author] became satisfied, that monarchy was a species of government essentially corrupt. He owed this conviction to the political writings of Swift and to a perusal of the Latin historians" (Preface, p. ix). James Arthur Preu points out that in Godwin's *Enquirer*, which belongs to the same period, there are twelve references to the number of pages read on a particular date in Swift's *Gulliver's Travels*. [32]

When Godwin wrote in Book V, Chapter vi, of *Political Justice*, that monarchy is founded in imposture and that its delusion is perpetuated by splendor and exaggeration, he may have had in mind Gulliver's visit to the court of Traldragdubh.[33] Gulliver reported:

I was commanded to crawl on my belly, and lick the floor as I advanced; but on account of my being a stranger, care was taken to have it made so clean that the dust was not offensive. However, this was a peculiar grace, not allowed to any but persons of the highest rank. . . . Nay sometimes the floor is strewed with dust on purpose. . . . And I have seen a great lord with his mouth so crammed, that when he had crept to the proper distance from the throne, he was not able to speak a word . . . when I had crept within four yards of the throne, I raised myself gently upon my knees, and then striking my forehead seven times on the ground I pronounced . . . the compliment established by the laws of the land for all persons admitted to the King's presence. It may be rendered into English thus: May your Celestial Majesty outlive the sun, eleven moons and a half.[34]

Godwin's reference in Book V, Chapter v, of *Political Justice* to the titles, ribands, and bribes given by monarchs to ensure complete obedience is reminiscent of Swift's Emperor of Lilliput who distributed red, green, and blue threads to whose whom he wished to honor.[35] Godwin saw kings as the victims of their faulty education. Accustomed to unquestioning obedience, they became impatient of any controls and unwilling to accept any limits to their power: "Being placed so high, they find but one step between them and the summit of social authority, and they cannot but eagerly desire to pass that step. Having so frequent occasions of seeing their commands implicitly obeyed, being trained in so long a scene of adulation and servility, it is impossible they should not feel some indignation, at the honest firmness that sets limits to their omnipotence" (Book V, Chapter iii). The little Emperor of Lilliput not only could not face the limitations of "honest firmness" at home, but would not rest content until he had become "the sole monarch of the whole world." [36]

When Godwin came to the connection between monarchy and war, he felt he could not improve on Swift's satiric description.

The usual causes of war are excellently described by Swift. "Sometimes the quarrel between two princes is to decide which of them shall dispossess a third of his dominions, where neither of them pretends to any right. Sometimes one prince quarrels with another, for fear the other should quarrel with him. . . . If a prince sends forces into a nation where the people are poor and ignorant, he may lawfully put half of them to death, and make slaves of the rest, in order to civilize and reduce them from their barbarous way of living. It is very kingly, honourable and frequent practice, when one prince desires the assistance of another to secure him against an invasion, that the assistant, when he has driven out the invader, should seize on the dominions himself, and kill, imprison or banish the prince he came to relieve" [37] (Book I, Chapter ii).

Godwin recounted the process by which "Ministers become a sort of miniature king in their turn. . . . There must be ministers of ministers, and a long beadroll of subordination, descending by tedious and complicated steps. Each of these lives on the smile of the minister, as he lives on the smile of the sovereign. . . . Each imitates the vices of his superior, and exacts from others the adulation he is obliged to pay" (Book V, Chapter v). Gulliver told the Lilliputian king that in his land "The Palace of a chief minister, is a seminary to breed up others in his own trade: the pages, lackeys, and porters, by imitating their master, become ministers of state in their several districts, and learn to excell in the three principal ingredients, of insolence, lying, and bribery." Godwin wrote that "To obtain honour, it will be thought necessary, by assiduity and intrigue, to make ourselves a party, to procure the recommendation of lords, and the good word of women of pleasure, and clerks in office" (Book V, Chapter v). And Swift described a chief minister as "usually governed by a decayed wench, or a favourite footman, who are the funnels through which all graces are conveyed, and may properly be called, in the last resort, the governors of the kingdom." [38] It was on the Island of Sorcerers, that Gulliver learned how much of the credit for government in a monarchy belongs to "bawds, whores, pimps, parasites, and buffoons . . ." [39]

Kings not only ignore merit, they cannot even bear the proximity of honest men. "From such intruders they hasten to men of pliant character, who will flatter their mistakes, put a varnish on their actions, and be visited by no scruples in assisting their appetites" (Book V, Chapter iii). Godwin may have learned this lesson from Gulliver's refusal to enslave the Blefuscuans merely that

Lilliput might gain a conquest. The Emperor immediately forgot Gulliver's spirited defense of his kingdom and resolved to destroy the monster who refused to gratify his appetite for greatness. And when Godwin laid siege to the entire "system of accumulated property," casting about for comrades in his intellectual crime, he wrote "Specimens of very powerful reasoning on the same side, may be found in *Gulliver's Travels,* particularly in Part IV, Chapter vi" (Book VIII, Chapter iii).

The second source of Godwin's conviction of the corruption of monarchy was Classical. Writing when the Republic was only a fading memory, the Latin historians found all their examples of virtue and liberty in the past, and their pages are full of the stories of the free, intrepid spirits who fought the rising tide of despotism. Sallust and Tacitus, Livy and Suetonius are replete with evidence of the bribery and corruption of despotism and the preference of monarchs for those counsellors who will flatter their fancies and encourage their vices.[40] It was Classical history that captured the attention of the boy who from his eleventh through his fifteenth year, ranged through the library of his tutor, Samuel Newton. "The works I read there with the greatest transport were the early volumes of the English translation of the *Ancient History* of Rollin. Few bosoms ever beat with greater ardour than mine did while perusing the grand struggle of the Greeks for independence against the assaults of the Persian despot; and this scene awakened a passion in my soul which will never cease but with life." [41]

The French Revolution, which erupted with the fall of the Bastille, July 14, 1789, ushered in Godwin's great work on political justice. English liberals greeted the Revolution with high enthusiasm and formed clubs and associations to express sympathy with the Revolution. They were optimistically certain that they would not cease until they had built the New "Jerusalem in England's green and pleasant land." [42] Corresponding societies were formed for the exchange of republican ideals. "My heart beat high with great swelling sentiments of Liberty," wrote Godwin.

I had been for nine years in principles a republican. I had read with great satisfaction the writing of Rousseau, Helvétius, and others, the most popular authors of France. I observed in them a system more general and simply philosophical than in the majority of English writers on political subjects; and I could not refrain from conceiving sanguine hopes of a revolution of which such writings had been the precursors. Yet I was far from approving all that I saw even in the commencement of the revolution. . . . I never for a moment ceased to disapprove of mob government and violence, and the impulses which men collected together in multitudes produce on each other. I desired such political changes only as should flow purely from the clear light of the understanding, and the erect and generous feelings of the heart.[43]

The same scruple that led him to reject Fox's offer of editorship of a Whig paper, the *Herald,* kept him from joining any of the radical corresponding societies. He had to maintain his personal independence of judgment against the mob, even when it was a liberal mob joined against tyranny. But he observed sympathetically and moved freely in the radical circles. Indeed he was present in the Old Jewry Meeting House, on November 4, 1780, when the Reverend Dr. Richard Price preached his famous sermon *A Discourse on the Love of Our Country* to the Friends of Liberty, of which Earl Stanhope was president. Dr. Price visualized with triumph "the ardour for liberty catching and spreading; a general amendment beginning in human affairs; the dominion of kings changed for the dominion of laws, and the dominion of priests giving way to the dominion of reason and conscience." [44]

When Thomas Paine's *Vindication of the Rights of Man* was published in 1791, Thomas Holcroft expressed vigorous sentiments that he evidently felt sure Godwin shared: "Not a single castration (Laud be unto God and J. S. Jordan!) can I discover— Hey for the New Jerusalem! The millennium! And peace and eternal beatitude be unto the soul of Thomas Paine." [45] Paine and Godwin, Holcroft and Wordsworth were all young men when the Bastille fell and "a strong shock was given to old opinions." They were enthusiastic young men in a time of which it might be said, "Bliss was it in that dawn to be alive, but to be young was very Heaven!" [46] Nor could Wordsworth's fellow-poet Southey forget, even after many years and many personal changes, the vision they saw in their youth: "Few persons but those who have lived in it can conceive or comprehend what the memory of the French Revolution was, nor what a visionary world seemed to open upon those who were just entering it. Old things seemed passing away, and nothing was dreamt of but the regeneration of the human race." [47]

> O times,
> In which the meagre, stale, forbidding ways
> Of custom, law, and statute, took at once
> The attraction of a country in romance!
> When Reason seemed the most to assert her rights
> When most intent on making of herself
> A prime enchantress—to assist the work,
> Which then was going forward in her name!
> Not favoured spots alone, but the whole Earth,
> The beauty wore of promise . . .[48]

When Godwin wrote that "individuals are every thing, and society, abstracted from the individuals of which it is composed, nothing" (Book V, Chapter xx), he was less a man of the eighteenth century, with its emphasis upon the general, the typical, and the representative, than a man of the early nineteenth century of the Romantic poets with their passionate individualism. If Wordsworth moved from the "degradation" of human society, the partiality of "custom," and the "impassioned sounds" of the time, to Nature, and stood serene and sure, "a sensitive being, a *creative* soul," Godwin's reliance was not upon a healing Nature, but upon the perfectible nature of man. He was convinced that "The inherent tendency of intellect is to improvement" (Book VIII, Chapter v). The one requirement of improvement was a society that placed supreme importance on the individual: "The proper method for hastening the decline of error, and producing uniformity of judgment, is not, by brute force, by laws, or by imitation; but, on the contrary, by exciting every man to think for himself . . ." (Book VIII, Chapter viii, Appendix). The extremity of his position is revealed when he says "We ought to be able to do without one another. He is the most perfect man, to whom society is not a necessity of life, but a luxury, innocent and enviable, in which he joyfully indulges" (Book VIII, Chapter viii, Appendix).

Godwin's odd combination of participation in and aloofness

from the political currents of his time was inevitable in the light of this individualism; he was no more a mere democrat, a believer in the rule of the many rather than the few, than were Oliver Cromwell and Jean Jacques Rousseau. In 1793 he called the fetish of majority rule "that intolerable insult upon all reason and justice—the deciding of truth by the counting up of numbers" (Book VIII, Chapter viii, Appendix). In his final book of essays, *Thoughts on Man,* written forty years later, he warned men that vote by ballot was potential mob-rule.[49]

In the great philosophical debate on man's ruling passion, Godwin had early taken a stand against the primacy of self-love and for the possibility of man's genuinely disinterested benevolence. Thus it seemed to him that governments were "very limited" in their "power of making men either virtuous or happy." But "let the most oppressed people under heaven once change their mode of thinking, and they are free." In Percy Bysshe Shelley's *Prometheus Unbound,* once Prometheus is able to forgive Zeus, Demogorgon (Godwin's doctrine of necessity) is set free to move the world on its appointed round of progress:

> And behold, thrones were kingless, and men walked
> One with the other even as spirits do,
> None fawned, none trampled; hate, disdain, or
>   fear,
> Self-love or self-contempt, on human brows
> No more inscribed,"
>   (Act III, Scene iii, lines 131-35.)

For both the poet and the political writer, once the mind of man is changed, the internal freedom must become the outward reality:

> To defy Power, which seems omnipotent;
> To love, and bear; to hope till Hope creates
> From its own wreck the thing it contemplates;
>   Neither to change, nor falter, nor repent;
> This, like thy glory, Titan, is to be
> Good, great and joyous, beautiful and free;
> This is alone Life, Joy, Empire, and Victory.
>   (Act IV, Lines 572-578.)

IV *Effect*

The fourth remarkable quality of the *Enquiry concerning Political Justice* is the effect it had upon its readers, an effect that con-
tinues in varying degree to the present. William Hazlitt summed
up the immediate reaction of almost stunned enthusiasm: "No
work in our time gave such a blow to the philosophical mind of
the country as the celebrated *Enquiry concerning Political Justice.*" [50] But he was by no means alone in this evaluation. Henry
Crabb Robinson recalled, even after a gap of many years, that "It
was in the spring of this year [1795], that I read a book which
gave a turn to my mind, and in effect directed the whole course of
my life—a book which after producing a powerful effect on the
youth of that generation, has now sunk into unmerited oblivion.
This was Godwin's *Political Justice.* . . . I entered fully into its
spirit, it left all others behind in my admiration, and I was willing
even to become a martyr for it." [51] Despite William Pitt's comment
in the Cabinet that "a three guinea book could not do much harm
in the class which was dangerous, precisely for want of guineas," [52]
the book had an immediate circulation of over four thousand
copies and, in many communities, was purchased as a joint effort
and shared by being read aloud to large local assemblies.

This was the early enthusiastic reaction in the Liberal period
immediately following the fall of the Bastille. The conservatives
were not at first actively hostile to the French Revolution and its
British progeny of association and enthusiasm, but by the year
1790 they began to recognize their danger. When, in November of
that year, Edmund Burke published his *Reflections on the French
Revolution,* he awakened conservative terror by denouncing the
French Revolution and by predicting that, unless its egalitarian
spirit and effects could be kept out of England, king, aristocracy,
church, and tradition might all well be carried away in a swelling
tide of democracy. The conservative reaction culminated very
quickly in the Aliens Act, the Seditious Meeting Act, the Treasonable Practices Act, and the suspension of *habeas corpus.* Only
then did the liberals recognize which way the tide was running,
and Thomas Paine's *Vindication of the Rights of Man,* of March
1791, was only one of some thirty-eight printed replies to Burke's
Reflections.

When Godwin reviewed the change in public attitude toward him and his works, he emphasized the fact that the publication of *Political Justice* had brought him such standing with the political and literary leaders of the time, as well as the host of young thinkers who were profoundly influenced by his writing and his friendship, that for more than four years he heard only "the voice of commendation." But when the idealism of the early Revolution was followed by the blood-bath of the guillotine, many of the former friends of "Liberty and Fraternity" began to fall away. Godwin's very consistency in principle made him an object of infamy to critics who had begun respectfully and judicially but who now grew hostile and insulting. He had no objection to the spirit of the Reverend Thomas Malthus' *Essay upon Population,* 1798, in which the clergyman countered Godwin's thesis that government is the chief obstacle to human happiness by advancing his own theory of over-population as the main cause of human misery. But in 1799 his former friend, Sir James Mackintosh, in a lecture entitled "The Law of Nature and Nations," treated him "like a highwayman or an assassin," and, according to Godwin, portrayed him "as a wretch, who only wanted the power in order to prove himself as infernal as Robespierre." The next year, 1800, the Reverend Robert Hall, an outstanding Baptist clergyman of the period, preached an eloquent sermon on "Modern Infidelity" which "outraged every notion of toleration or decorum" and which singled out for particular attack the political radicalism of Godwin and his followers. Then in April of that same year, Dr. Samuel Parr, a close and fatherly friend of Godwin, was invited to deliver the Spital Sermon before the Lord Mayor of London and a distinguished congregation of the city; Dr. Parr took particular aim at Godwin's doctrine of universal benevolence, which he condemned as destructive of the entire moral order. Godwin's bleakly courteous reply shows that this defection of friendship hurt far more than "the vulgar buffoonery and scandal to the amount of half a score, and British critics, Anti-Jacobin newspapers, and Anti-Jacobin magazines without number." [53] The growing hostility to Godwin extended to his friends. Henry Crabb Robinson, who had received *Political Justice* so enthusiastically, publicly defended it so warmly that even two years afterward, when he visited friends at Bury, their pastor, the same Reverend Robert Hall, had anticipated his visit and urged his parishioners to show no hospitality to so dangerous and infectious a doctrinaire.[54]

Burke, of course, thundered against the political tract as "Pure defecated Atheism, the brood of that putrid carcase the French Revolution." [55] But even the gentle adulation of Godwin's young disciple, Percy Bysshe Shelley, must have been bitter-sweet when, in his first letter of 1812, he admitted that he was thrilled and surprised to learn that the great political philosopher still lived: "I had enrolled your name in the list of the honourable dead. I had felt regret that the glory of your being had passed from this earth of ours." [56]

William Hazlitt pungently outlined the reaction against Godwin in *The Spirit of the Age: or Contemporary Portraits:*

The Spirit of the Age was never more fully shown than in its treatment of this writer—its love of paradox and change, its dastard submission to prejudice and to the fashion of the day. Five-and-twenty years ago he was in the very zenith of a sultry and unwholesome popularity; he blazed as a sun in the firmament of reputation; no one was more talked of, more looked up to, more sought after, and wherever liberty, truth, justice was the theme, his name was not far off—now he has sunk below the horizon, and enjoys the serene twilight of a doubtful immortality . . . he is to all ordinary intents and purposes dead and buried. . . ." [57]

CHAPTER 3

The Writer in Many Roles

"They say that thou wert lovely from thy birth,
  Of glorious parents thou the aspiring child;
I wonder not—for One then left this earth
  Whose life was like a setting planet mild,
  Which clothed thee in the radiance undefiled
Of its departing glory; still her fame
  Shines on thee, through the tempests dark and wild
Which shake these latter days; and thou canst claim
The shelter, from thy Sire, of an immortal name."

PERCY BYSSHE SHELLEY, from "To
Mary [Shelley]," Dedication to
The Revolt of Islam

WILLIAM Godwin met Samuel Taylor Coleridge in 1794, after Coleridge had included a sonnet to Godwin in a letter to Robert Southey. It was a propitious beginning to an acquaintance which Godwin described as having ripened into a "high degree of affectionate intimacy" by 1800.[1] But the great talker and the great listener somehow jarred upon each other at their first meeting. Coleridge had praised Godwin in poetry as one who was

     . . . form'd t'illume a sunless world forlorn,
       As o'er the chill and dusky brow of Night,
       In Finland's wintry skies the Mimic Morn
     Electric pours a stream of rosy light,

     Pleas'd I have mark'd OPPRESSION, terror-pale,
       Since, thro' the windings of her dark machine,
       Thy steady eye has shot its glances keen—
     And bade th' All-lovely 'scenes at distance hail.'

> Nor will I not thy holy guidance bless,
>   And hymn thee, GODWIN! with an ardent lay;
>   For that thy voice, in Passion's stormy day,
> When wild I roam'd the bleak Heath of Distress,
>
> Bade the bright form of Justice meet my way—
> And told me that her name was HAPPINESS.[2]

Perhaps this high praise of the author of *Political Justice* came from not having read the book before the sonnet was written, for after their first interview, the poet denounced, in highly Coleridgean prose, the "grossness and vulgar insanocecity of this dim-headed prig of a philosophocide." [3]

Nevertheless, Godwin considered Coleridge as a pivotal influence upon his life and opinions, because, from conversations with Coleridge in 1800, he dated his shift from Holcroft's atheism to Coleridge's vague theism that consisted, for Godwin, in the "reverent and soothing contemplation of all that is beautiful, grand, or mysterious in the system of the universe." [4] And in the following year, when Coleridge read Godwin's reply to the accusation of rationalistic anarchism in Dr. Parr's *Spital Sermon,* he used the margin of his copy of the pamphlet to confess: "They reflect great honor on Godwin's head and heart. Tho' I did it only in the zenith of his reputation, yet I feel remorse *ever* to have spoken unkindly of such a man." [5]

The ups and downs of the Coleridge relationship illustrate in a single instance what was happening generally to Godwin's standing and reputation in the years that lay between the publication of *Political Justice* in 1793 and the final refuge in the editorship of books for children. This chapter will attempt to follow the writer through the period of declining reputation, in his varied roles as preacher, pamphleteer, defender (of himself and others), husband, friend, and essayist.

I *Preacher*

There is no such spirited picture of Godwin in the pulpit as Hazlitt's description of Coleridge—"an eagle dallying with the wind." There is only *Sketches of History, in Six Sermons,* published in 1784, and the autobiographical hints of the vast erosion of his theological faith in his fragmentary journals. T. Cadell published the small volume of sermons on the same financial terms as Murray's publication of the *Herald of Literature*—Godwin gained nothing. Dedicated to Dr. Richard Watson, the liberal Bishop of Llandaff, Godwin's *Sketches* contained a sermon on the character of Aaron, one on Hazael, and four on Jesus. It could scarcely be called a high mark of nonconformist pulpit oratory, yet it is marked by the characteristic Godwin lucidity of style and clarity of meaning. Out of simple, straightforward statements the sermons occasionally rise to exalted and eloquent prose. The precision of the French essayists is the basic pattern for style, manner, and meaning. Preached by a supposedly staunch Calvinist or Sandemanian, Sermon I gives a clue to the future, when Godwin states categorically, "God Himself has no right to be a tyrant." The same sermon captures the mildness of the man that always accompanied the vigor of his statements: "May we all of us exemplify the quietness of an Aaron, and the unresentful mildness of a redeemer, that so we may be united with these great and illustrious characters for ever hereafter." The last four sermons make it clear that Godwin was far more deeply stirred by Jesus as Son of Man than as Son of God.

The fragmentary notes Godwin made during the years from 1772 to 1795 record that while still in college at Hoxton he "was persuaded there was more virtue and less crime in the best ages of Greece and Rome than in any period of the Christian dispensation, and was therefore satisfied that the doctrine of eternal punishment in hell was not absolutely required to prevent men from running out into excesses that would be destructive of the social system." Before entering the Dissenting College at Hoxton, the young theologue had become a Tory in politics and a Sandemanian in religion. He managed to defend both positions vigorously during the collegiate years. But "I had, however, no sooner gone out into the world than my sentiments on both these points began to give way; my tory-ism did not survive above a year, and between my twenty-third and my twenty-fifth year my religious creed insensibly degenerated on the heads of the Trinity, eternal torments, and some others." [6]

Until 1782 he was a firm believer in the doctrine of Calvin that the "majority of mankind were objects of divine condemnation, and that their punishment would be everlasting." But Baron d'Holbach's *Système de la Nature,* which he read that year, converted him to Deism. The next year he read Dr. Joseph Priestley's *Institutes of the Christian Religion,* and the Deist became a Socinian. Two years later, Socinianism had eroded to the point that he corresponded with Dr. Priestley about his dwindling faith. In two more years, 1787, he describes himself as "a complete unbeliever." [7]

An undated note in his journals traces his descent into atheism and his eventual re-emergence as a Coleridgean theist:

In my thirty-first year I became acquainted with Mr. Thomas Holcroft, and it was probably in consequence of our mutual conversations that I became two years after an unbeliever, and in my thirty-sixth year an atheist.

In my forty-fourth year I ceased to regard the name of Atheist with the same complacency I had done for several preceding years, at the same time retaining the utmost repugnance of understanding for the idea of an intelligent Creator and Governor of the universe, which strikes my mind as the most irrational and ridiculous anthropomorphism. My theism, if such I may be permitted to call it, consists in a reverent and soothing contemplation of all that is beautiful, grand, or mysterious in the system of the universe, and in a certain conscious intercourse and correspondence with the principles of these attributes, without attempting the idle task of developing and defining it—into this train of thinking I was first led by conversations of S. T. Coleridge.[8]

Godwin made a sharp distinction between a natural and a beautiful religion of pantheism which sees God in nature and "endows every object of sense with a living soul," and a "detestable" and "hag-rid" religion which torments with "phantoms of guilt," "endows the priest with his pernicious empire over the mind," "undermines boldness of opinion and intrepidity in feeling," "aggravates the inevitable calamity of death," and "haunts us with the fiends and retributory punishments of a future world." [9] His personal religion at last became a kind of humanism. In a most complacent letter to his mother he wrote, "My views, I think, were always right, but they are now nobler and more exalted. I am in every respect, so far as I am able to follow the dictates of my own mind, perfectly indifferent to all personal gratification. I know of nothing worth the living for but usefulness and the service of my fellow-creatures. The only object I pursue is to increase, as far as lies in my power, the quantity of their knowledge and goodness and happiness." [10]

II *Pamphleteer and Defender*

In 1793, the same year in which Godwin published *Political Justice,* a convention was held in Edinburgh to demand annual parliaments and universal male suffrage. Several of the English and Scottish reformers who attended the meeting were brought to trial in Scotland, convicted of seditious activity, and sentenced to long terms of transportation. Informers and government spies were in every large gathering. The courts became more drastic; *Habeas Corpus* was suspended. The government decided it was time to move vigorously against the corresponding societies which had sprung up to welcome the first idealistic period of the French Revolution. Thomas Holcroft, who with Horne Tooke, John Thelwall, Thomas Hardy, and other associates, had formed the Constitutional and the London Corresponding Societies, along with eight people of similar mind and activity, were arrested and placed in the Tower of London. When the case came to trial in October, 1794, Lord Chief Justice Eyre gave to the grand jury a charge which Godwin described in his pamphlet *Cursory Strictures,* as a "sound and constitutional exposition" of the traditional laws concerning treason in its first part; in the second part a "portentous speculation" concerning a new treason which was no treason at all—"conspiring to subvert the Monarchy." Even the judge admitted that the charge might have ended at this point, but the third section moved into the realm of "hypothesis, presumption, prejudication, and conjecture." [11] The Chief Justice referred to two forms of treason under which the accused might well be found guilty: association to change the constitution of the House of Commons, and "the project of a Convention to be assembled under the advice and direction of some of these associations." [12]

Godwin finds the judge guilty of what he calls "incroachment." It is "a proceeding, by which an affirmation is modestly insinuated at first, accompanied with considerable doubt and qualification; repeated afterwards, and accompanied with these qualifications; and at last asserted in the most peremptory and arrogant terms." [13]

And in a savage peroration he writes a closing speech and sentence for the Chief Justice:

He has already admitted, that there is no law of precedent for their condemnation. If therefore he address them in the frank language of sincerity, he must say, "Six months ago you engaged in measures, which you believed conducive to the public good. You examined them in the full conviction of the understanding. You adopted them from this ruling motive, the love of your country and mankind. . . . And for this, the Sentence of the Court (but not of the law) is, 'That you, and each of you, shall be taken from the bar, and conveyed to the place from whence you came, and from thence be drawn upon a hurdle to the place of execution, there to be hanged by the neck, but not until you are dead; you shall be taken down alive, your privy members shall be cut off, and your bowels shall be taken out and burnt before your faces; your heads shall be severed from your bodies, and your bodies shall then be divided into four quarters, which are to be at the King's disposal; and the Lord have mercy on your souls!' " [14]

The pamphlet from which this peroration was quoted, William Godwin's *Cursory Strictures on the Charge Delivered by Lord Chief Justice Eyre to the Grand Jury, October 2, 1794*, was first published in the *Morning Chronicle* of October 21 and then printed and sold by Daniel Isaac Eaton, at the Cock and Swine. It was through these cursory strictures by "A Lover of Order" (pseudonym of Godwin), that Hardy, Tooke, and Thelwall were found not guilty and the government abandoned the prosecutions. Thomas Holcroft, thus liberated, crossed the court and took his seat beside his literary champion, William Godwin; and Sir Thomas Lawrence made a sketch of the two men in profile—a stooped, reflective Godwin contrasting with a belligerent, stern Holcroft.[15]

Cursory Strictures is a brilliant brief that would have raised any fledgling barrister to the height of his profession, but it was not written by a lawyer. Instead of imparting legal fame, it damaged the reputation of the writer. Nevertheless, it became one of the deciding factors in the high-treason trials of 1794, and quite probably it saved the lives of twelve public-spirited Englishmen.[16] One evening, when Godwin was a dinner guest at the home of Horne Tooke, there was much teasing and cross-examination about the identity of "A Lover of Order." When Godwin finally acknowledged the authorship, Tooke "took his hand, and pressed it to his lips, saying 'I can do no less for the hand that saved my life!' " [17]

In the fall of the following year, 1795, Parliament was debating a Treasonable Practices bill and a Seditious Meetings bill, both of which subsequently became law. Godwin wrote a carefully reasoned refutation entitled *Considerations on Lord Grenville's and Mr. Pitt's Bills, Concerning Treasonable and Seditious Practices, and Unlawful Assemblies, By a Lover of Order*. In accord with the basic principles of his *Political Justice*, Godwin argued that "the great problem of political knowledge, is, how to preserve to mankind the advantages of freedom, together with an authority, strong enough to control every daring violation of general security and peace." [18] He points out that the Corresponding Societies simply echo the desire of all men to reform the inequities of law and government. But he offends all his friends who belong to such groups by characterizing their meetings as "an appeal to the passions," and he espouses an almost Burkean philosophy of political gradualism: reform which is "carried on by slow, almost insensible steps, and by just degrees." [19]

At the heart of his argument, he grants that it was the duty of government to protect itself by timely measures against violent disruption, just as he grants that the activities of radical groups may well give cause for serious alarm. Nevertheless, he considers the measures suggested by Lord Grenville and Mr. Pitt as going beyond all reasonable punitive techniques and as becoming in their turn a cause for the most serious alarm to all lovers of freedom:[20] "Lord Grenville's bill relates to the most important of all human affairs, the liberty of the press. Mr. Pitt's bill touches upon one of the grand characteristics of English liberty, the fundamental provision of the bill of rights, the right of the subject to consult respecting grievances, and to demand redress." [21] After pointing out that even David Hume, hated by Republicans, could have been prosecuted under such a law, Godwin considers his own case:

Who does not see, that, if I write a pamphlet or book in which any political question is treated or incidentally mentioned, I may suffer the penalties of this act? Who does not see, that, if the king's minister do not like my pamphlet, or do not like my face, if he have an old grudge against me for any past proceeding, if I have not proved a fortunate candidate for his general good-will, or if, by any distortion of under-standing, or excessiveness of alarm, he be led to see in my pamphlet things it does not contain, I may suffer the penalties of this act? [22]

Godwin can hardly believe that a Christian clergyman, Bishop Horsley, a member of the committee for the bill from the House of Lords, could say on November 11 that he did not know "what the mass of the people in any country had to do with the laws, but to obey them." Then, almost in a direct reference to Godwin's writings, the Bishop admitted that "philosophical disquisitions might be still written and published, though he always thought they did more harm than good." [23] Godwin's pamphlet ends on a surprising note of prophetic hope: "The enthusiastic advocates for liberty are too apt to exclaim upon every new encroachment, 'This is the last degree of hostility; everything depends upon our present success; if we miscarry now, the triumph of despotism is final, and there is no longer any hope that remains to us.' The precisely opposite of this is the true inference in the present in-stance. These bills are *an unwilling homage, that the too eager ad-vocates of authority pay to the rising genius of freedom.*" [24]

William Godwin staunchly defended the dedication to freedom of his friends, but, to all the attacks on his own character and convictions, he made but one reply, the *Thoughts Occasioned by the Perusal of Dr. Parr's Spital Sermon* (1801). Godwin and the eminent Whig Divine, Dr. Samuel Parr, had been friends for many years, but at the end of 1799, a coolness settled upon the relationship, perhaps as the result of a harshly critical onslaught on the clergy in the *Enquirer*. At any rate, when Godwin visited at Hatton, in the company of Basil Montagu, Doctor Parr had evidently not seen the critical essay, and all was well. [25] But, when Godwin sent a copy of *St. Leon* to Hatton, he received neither acknowledgement nor reply. Godwin wrote a letter to Parr on January 3, 1800. To the letter there came no reply, but a reply with a vengeance came on the following Easter Tuesday, April 15, 1800. Dr. Parr was honored by the invitation to preach the annual Spital Sermon before the Lord Mayor and a large and distin-guished congregation of London leaders. [26] He chose the occasion to castigate most thoroughly and recognizably the adherents of what he designated "the new philosophy."

To the direct and unmistakable reference to himself and *Political Justice,* Godwin wrote a reply which was remarkable for dignity, sorrow, and restraint. He pointed out that the time when Parr chose to attack him was an hour in which Jacobinism was already discredited and the public cry against him "had already become loud and numerous." [27] Godwin was deeply aware of the irony by which he had been bitterly resented by the radicals in the liberal period because he would not join them completely in their radical activities. His pamphlet *Considerations on Lord Grenville's and Mr. Pitt's Bills* censured the impassioned popular lectures of his friend John Thelwall and the activities of the London Corresponding Society, which, no matter how high their purpose and ideal, were "calculated sooner or later to bring on scenes of confusion." [28] But in the period of the conservative reaction, the very friends who had censured him before for his revolutionary lukewarmness, now accused him of revolutionary sympathies: "I never went so far, in my partiality for the practical principles of the French Revolution as many of those with whom I was accustomed to converse. I uniformly declared myself an enemy to revolution. Many persons censured me for this lukewarmness; I willingly endured the censure. Several of those persons are now gone into the opposite extreme. They must excuse me; they have wandered wide of me on the one side and on the other; I did not follow them before; I cannot follow them now." [29]

Humbly, he describes himself as writing the *Enquiry concerning Political Justice* "in the innocence of my heart," not at all sure of the truth of his own system, but faithful to the speculative spirit which had led him far out of the beaten track. The value of these speculations would have to be assessed and assigned by their readers. "Unprophetic as I was, I rested in perfect tranquillity"; and at first his faith was richly rewarded with intellectual leadership and acclamation far beyond anything he could have anticipated. It is not surprising then, that he confesses he never dreamed that in a few short years he would "be dragged to public odium, and made an example to deter all future enquirers from the practice of unshackled speculation. I was no man of the world; I was a mere student, connected with no party, elected into no club, exempt from every imputation of political conspiracy or cabal." [30]

As was occasionally the case with Godwin's prose, his muted defence rose into the swelling tones of social millennial prophecy. The prophet was of no importance; the prophecy raised a question of the highest magnitude ever "brought before the tribunal of the public. . . . Are vice and misery, as my antagonists so earnestly maintain, in all their extent, and with all their disgustful circumstances as they now exist in the world, entailed on us forever; or may we hope ultimately to throw off, or greatly diminish, the burthen? In other cases of an eminent nature, what the heart of man is able to conceive, the hand of man is strong enough to perform. . . . For myself I firmly believe that days of greater virtue and more ample justice will descend upon the earth. . . ." [31]

III   *Husband and Father*

The remarkable story of Mary Wollstonecraft is widely known and has titillated many a generation. Briefly, Mary met Captain Gilbert Imlay, an American living in Paris. He had taken part in the Revolutionary War and had become a commissioner for laying out land tracts in pioneer areas of the United States. An attractive person, but a speculator without any personal fortune, his main achievement was a model monograph entitled *A Topographical Description of the Western Territory of North America.*[32] At the time they met, Mary had come to the conclusion that marriage was simply mutual affection, and that, when that affection was gone, the marriage no longer existed. Thus they lived together in Paris, from August, 1793, until he was called to Havre on business. There Mary joined him and gave birth to Fanny (named for her dearest friend, Fanny Blood) in 1794. When business called Imlay to London, Mary returned to Paris and later became his business representative in Sweden and Norway, with credentials stating ". . . I, Gilbert Imlay, citizen of the United States of America, at present residing in London, do nominate, constitute, and appoint Mary Imlay, my best friend and wife, to take the sole management and direction of all my affairs. . . ." [33] When she returned to London, Imlay offered to settle an annuity on her for the support of the child. She scornfully rejected the offer, but rejoined him for Fanny's sake. However, when she discovered an *affaire d'amour* under the same roof, she leaped from Putney Bridge in an unsuccessful attempt to drown herself.

Two years later Godwin met Mary at a party in honor of Thomas Paine. Paine was reticent and Mary voluble, so Godwin recalled her as the woman who talked too much.[34] By early 1797 this estimate was revised sufficiently to permit a liaison, with Godwin taking rooms twenty doors down the street from her residence in Somers Town. On March 29, 1797, the union was legalized by a brief, private service in Old St. Pancras Church, an event Godwin omitted to mention in his diary. Five months later an expectant Mary wrote a hopeful and impatient note to Godwin: "I have no doubt of seeing the animal today; but must wait for Mrs. Blenkinsop (midwife to the Westminster Lying-In Hospital) to guess at the hour. . . ." And later the same day, "Still at present she thinks I shall not immediately be freed from my load." [35] The "animal" was not the William so confidently anticipated, but Mary (afterwards Mrs. Shelley), born at twenty minutes past eleven that night. In spite of all the doctors could do, the mother died the following Sunday morning, September 10, at twenty minutes before eight o'clock.[36]

When William Godwin published the *Memoirs of Mary Wollstonecraft Godwin* (1798), its frank statement of Mary's relationships with both Imlay and Godwin, and its restrainedly beautiful account of their love for each other, seemed to many people to confirm their suspicion that the arguments of the new philosophers were simply ingenious sophistries designed to sanction the most abandoned licentiousness. The August 1801 issue of the *Anti-Jacobin* quipped in verse,

> Being her spouse, he tells, with huge delight,
> How oft she cuckolded the silly clown,
> And lent, O lovely piece! herself to half the town.[37]

And the same year, in his novel *The Infernal Quixote,* Charles Lucas described Godwin's memoir of Mary as "The History of the Intrigues of His Own Wife." [38]

By the publication of his memoir, and the posthumous publication of her novelistic tract *The Wrongs of Woman,* Godwin made it apparent that his influence had deepened her radicalism; she steadily became, under his tutelage, more sympathetic with his attitude toward marriage, and more defiant and uncompromising in her own attitude toward what people considered the basic institutions of society. In this posthumous novel, Mary Wollstonecraft protested against the economic conditions that discouraged decent employment for women and made prostitution almost inevitable. She pled for more liberal divorce laws whereby a woman might be set free from the life-long tyranny of a drunkard or a dissipated rake. She described, with approval, a wife who deserted her low husband to join a far more intellectual, moral person. Her former low estate was legally acceptable; her new, higher relationship was socially forbidden. But to many readers the logic of her desertion seemed to shake the foundations of social morality.

The personal hatred felt for the author of *Political Justice* was only deepened by the championship of his friends who sympathized with his advocacy of greater freedom between the sexes and who, sometimes more frankly than their master, defended his position. In 1796, Mary Hays, a long-time friend and admirer of Mary Wollstonecraft, whose own reputation had suffered by that connection, published the *Memoirs of Emma Courtney*. In this novel the heroine, who has been taught individualism by *Political Justice* and feminine independency by *A Vindication of the Rights of Woman*, becomes the mistress of a man she admires and loves, only to suffer the usual clashes with the established code of social and religious ethics. The rebellious spirit of the novel made it clear that, instead of preaching the usual sermon on the "wages of sin," the author flaunts an approval of both the books and the lives of William Godwin and Mary Wollstonecraft.[39]

The widowed father of a half-daughter Fanny and a full daughter Mary was seated one evening on the balcony of his home. Out of the evening coolness rose the adoring voice of his next-door-neighbor, fluting the irresistible question, "Is it possible that I behold the immortal Godwin?" The lonely, perplexed widower yielded to the worshipful initiative of Mary Jane Clairmont and took her to be his wife, along with her daughter, Jane "Claire" Clairmont, destined to literary notoriety as the mistress of George Gordon, Lord Byron, and as the heiress of some of her mother's own initiative. Even the gentle Charles Lamb called the new Mrs.

Godwin "that damned Mrs. Godwin" and that "disgusting woman who wears green spectacles." But, damned or disgusting, she worked steadily by Godwin's side through years of public hostility when he dared not use his own name as author of a book, through steadily approaching bankruptcy, through the tedious chores of translations and publication of children's books, the humiliating button-holing of friends, and the final ironic harbor of the old radical as sinecure "yeoman usher of the Exchequer." [40]

Mary Jane Clairmont Godwin seems to have been a good mother to their son William and certainly an indulgent one to Jane, whom she clearly felt should have all the advantages their declining means could afford, while Fanny and Mary were relegated to the status of household drudges, roles from which one would emerge an illicit Cinderella, and the other a suicide. After a somewhat stormy youth and a perilously long period of various attempts at a career, the young William settled down to be a parliamentary reporter for the *Morning Chronicle* and a fairly successful draughtsman. Following his deeply-lamented death in the autumn of 1832, his father published his novel *Transfusion,* with a touchingly restrained memoir.[41]

IV *Friend*

William Godwin looked into his own character and mused: "I am bold and adventurous in opinions, not in life; it is impossible that a man with my diffidence and embarrassment should be. This, and perhaps only this, renders me often cold, uninviting, and unconciliating in society. . . ." [42] Such wry self-analysis goes far to explain why Leslie Stephen wrote, "Nobody would ask for an hour of William Godwin. His most obvious qualities, a remorseless 'ergotism,' squeezing the last drop out of an argument; a frigid dogmatism, not redeemed by the fervour which half excuses fanaticism; and a singular incapacity for even suspecting the humourous aspects of life, are qualities which go far to make the superlative bore." [43] It may also explain why his early biographer Charles Kegan Paul felt that "It would not be fair to suppress these very characteristic notes of hot temper, and quarrels with his best friends, which also appear only too often in the letters." [44]

John Middleton Murry preferred to find the clue to the apparent paradoxes of Godwin's ideals and his manners in what he calls his "two scales of value: one, for those who understood and belonged to the new world, another for those who did not. From those who did, or professed to understand, he desired no homage, because what he had revealed to them was not his own; from those who did not, criticism and injustice and abuse were meaningless." [45] The acute eyes of William Hazlitt had recorded "his foible to fawn on those who used him cavalierly and to be cavalier to those who express an undue or unqualified admiration of him." [46] Murry felt that Godwin's contemporary caught the problem, but that he himself had discovered the explanation. Yet the "cold, uninviting, boring, greedy, impecunious" William Godwin was loved dearly by Mary Wollstonecraft, enjoyed the invincible loyalty of his children, and was unfailingly generous to the claims of an unending procession of young men who looked to him for the warm counsel and selfless service of a lover of youth.

There are many letters from the year 1801 alone, which give eloquent testimony to the great attraction Godwin exerted upon talented and remarkable men much younger than he. Using the ex-clergyman as a secular priest, they confessed their difficulties as well as their hopes and dreams for rich and useful lives. Charles Kegan Paul, whose *William Godwin: His Friends and Contemporaries* is still the best source for Godwin's letters and diaries, mentions the discovery of a large number of these intimate and confessional letters from young men. Paul assumes that Godwin neglected to destroy them before his death and that they were simply bundled together with other less private papers. The names are now mostly meaningless and the letters of no literary or historical significance. But their existence is important because ". . . it is desirable to notice the fact that such outpourings of spirit were made to Godwin, if we would understand what he really was who seemed to some only the unimpassioned philosopher, but who yet was to those who could get beyond his shell the eager, sympathetic man, who had not forgotten the days of his own youth." [47]

The number of young men whom Godwin helped at critical and formative periods of their lives is legion: Willis Webb and Thomas Cooper, John Arnot and Henry Rosser, James Marshall and George Dyson, James Ballantyne, James Bell, and William Cooke, to name only a few. When Willis Webb left Eton and prepared to go to a large private school at Hitcham, Godwin received him into his lodgings as pupil and member of the family. This first of his "young men" later wrote devotedly to Godwin during his student years at St. John's College, Cambridge University. Thomas Cooper, later one of the most distinguished actors of the early American theater, was taken into the philosopher's household at the age of twelve. His father had died in the East Indies, and Cooper turned to Godwin, in the summer of 1788, as to a very distant relative upon whom he had actually no claim. Out of his own real poverty, Godwin fed, clothed, and carefully educated the homeless lad.[48] That it was often a stormy and perhaps thankless relationship is indicated by a fragment of a letter Godwin sent Cooper, April 19, 1790: "I am poor, and with considerable labour maintain my little family; yet I am willing to spend my money upon your wants and pleasures. My time is of the utmost value to me, yet I bestow a large portion of it upon your improvement. . . . If I can contribute to make you virtuous and respectable hereafter, I do not care whether I then possess your friendship, I am contented you should hate me." [49]

A young man who turned to him both to be helped and to help was Francis Place. Because Place knew how much Godwin needed money and how richly the hard-working, influential author deserved help, and because he accepted the political moralist's dictum that it was the privilege of wealthy men to assist men of genius and thus disperse accumulated and hereditary wealth, he became Godwin's financial assistant. But, when Place reached the point that his family complained that further gifts would endanger their own economic security, he discontinued his help. Now Godwin had imagined that he was dealing with a man who genuinely accepted the principle of "universal benevolence," and who was ready—without limiting the freedom of the recipient or expecting the gratitude that corrupts men's sense of honor and judgment—to help a man of genius until he reached the level of prosperity of the donor, and only then to discontinue his aid. But the world emphatically pronounced Place overgenerous and Godwin grasping and ungrateful. Thus Place himself began to feel that Godwin ought not to have expected so much. The odd thing is that the general critical verdict is almost always on the side of Francis Place and rarely on the side of Godwin. Yet it is Godwin who was consistent with principle and the initial understanding of the transaction, and it is Place who fell away from an ideal to a worldly judgment.

Godwin wrote that in 1792 he "acquired the friendship of many excellent persons—Thomas Wedgwood, Richard Porson, Joseph Gerald, Robert Murry, and Joseph Ritson." [50] In Wedgwood he acquired another Maecenas who was willing to limit his personal expenses in order that he might have more money to spare for others. With extraordinary tenacity of purpose, the china manufacturer applied his dangerous generosity to men of high promise —Godwin, Wordsworth, and many others. The correspondence of Godwin and Wedgwood is remarkably equable, marred only by the patron's illnesses and by his insight that he might sacrifice to lend but that he must not lose all peace of mind by having a recipient move into his home and life. In 1807, when it became necessary for Godwin to move from the small shop in Hanway Street to larger publishing quarters in Skinner Street, Holborn, a number of old friends, and many new readers of his works came forward with loans or gifts; conspicuous among these were Sir Francis Burdett and Lords Holland, Selkirk, and Lauderdale.[51]

Probably the most tempestuous of his friends was John Thelwall, an early agitator for parliamentary reform. He wrote pamphlets and gave popular lectures fearlessly castigating the government and upholding the standard of French liberalism. Tried for treason in 1794, he was acquitted along with Thomas Hardy and Horne Tooke. He immediately began lecturing again, until Pitt and Grenville, in utter exasperation, succeeded in muzzling him with the 1795 bill for the suppression of sedition. When the liberal voice was finally silenced, Burke expressed his satisfaction in "A Letter to a Noble Lord," and the *Anti-Jacobin* of April 9, 1798, crowed loudly. Tracked by government spies and persecuted by the frantic fear of the conservatives, he yet managed to find friends like Samuel Taylor Coleridge and William Wordsworth. The latter used Thelwall's early poem *The Peripatetic* (1793) as the framework of *The Excursion.*[52]

Although Godwin and Thelwall were friends, and Godwin had defended him at the trials of 1794, he always disapproved of his revolutionary ardor. At the trial, a government spy and informer named John Taylor testified that at one of Thelwall's lectures

Thelwall had read with approval a number of passages from Godwin's *Political Justice*. But when Thelwall was in the Tower awaiting trial, Godwin refused to visit him on the ground that, as some danger was involved in such a visit, he was willing to sacrifice the personal pleasure to the greater utility of preserving his freedom to contribute to the larger public weal. Godwin's stern consistency must not have been very pleasing, yet it was clearly contagious, because in a later lecture, Thelwall argued that it was his duty to continue his task of spreading truth even though he was grief-stricken at the recent death of his mother. The following year, 1795, Thelwall quarreled bitterly with Godwin when the latter censured the lectures of his friend, whom he called "an impatient and headlong reformer," and criticized the London Corresponding Society as "calculated sooner or later to bring on scenes of confusion"; yet Thelwall recognized that in Godwin's seeming reversal there was a central integrity and devotion to principle.[53]

Samuel Taylor Coleridge lauded the author of *Political Justice* in 1794, but the following year, after having read the book, he attacked its principles in the Bristol lectures, and in *The Watchman*, in 1796. During the same period, William Wordsworth was first elated with the promise of Godwinian perfectionism, but later plunged into pessimism at what appeared to him its failure. He retired to Racedown, Dorsetshire, to clarify his spiritual problems and to salvage what was left of his faith in reason and the capacity of man for perpetual self-improvement. Out of intellectual turmoil, he wrote *The Borderers*, which, in some sense, was a repudiation of Godwinian optimism.[54]

One of the longest-term friendships of Godwin's life was that with Thomas Holcroft, the man most influential in Godwin's rejection of Christian doctrine. They exulted together over Tom Paine's *Rights of Man*, and later they put their heads together over the task of revising it for a new edition. When Holcroft was committed to Newgate Prison on the charge of high treason, he immediately called for Godwin's help and was not disappointed—Godwin's pamphlet set Holcroft free and forced the prosecution to drop proceedings against others arrested on the same charge.[55]

Melancholy entries in Godwin's Journal for November 8-17 (1789) and a letter written November 18, 1789, to John Fenwick (Lamb's "Bigod" in *Essays of Elia*), give cryptic evidence of God-

win's involvement in the life of his friend Holcroft. "Nov. 8. Sun.
Dine at Holcroft's—*Elopement de son fils*. 9. M. to Gravesend. 15.
Sun. Dine at Holcroft's; Set out for Deal. Call upon Crosdil. W.
Holcroft. 16. M. *Mort de son fils*. 17. T. *Funerailles;* to have drank
tea with Holcroft at Miss Williams." The brief entries of the Journal, amplified by the letter, explain that Godwin was actually
within hearing of the suicide shot, when his friend's runaway son,
in terror and panic at the pursuit of his father, killed himself
aboard the *Fame*, a ship which later sailed to the West Indies.[56]

When he was middle-aged, and seemed to many methodical,
cold, and formal, he still continued to attract young men of adventurous spirit and personal talent, and he never failed to receive
them with kindness. One such was a young Scot named John Arnot.[57] In 1819, Henry Blanch Rosser, a new young friend, was his
frequent guest and companion on his walks.[58] James Marshall and
George Dyson were two other young men who found in him an
inspiring mind and a warm friendliness. James Ballantyne, the
Edinburgh printer, and Dr. James Bell were deeply impressed by
and attracted to Godwin, when they were young.[59] And in 1834, at
the age of seventy-eight, we find Godwin referring to still another
"new young friend," William Cooke.[60]

By 1813, at the very time Crabb Robinson informs us that Godwin was a living legend, though almost a social pariah, the philosopher received a letter from a new disciple—one who had the
power to clothe the philosophical principles of *Political Justice* in
the beauty of undying poetry—Percy Bysshe Shelley.[61] It was
about the year 1811 that Shelley first came under the intellectual
sway of Godwinism, and imagined that he had finally found the
master who could lead him into a hopeful resolution of his doubts
and fears. On the third of January, 1812, Shelley wrote his shyly
bold first letter to Godwin. He recognized that he was overstep-
ping "the limits of custom's prescription" in endeavoring "to form
a friendship with William Godwin." [62] At first he had assumed that
the great thinker was no longer alive. When he found he was living, he struck a Shelleyan note that Godwin would have appreci-
ated by remarking that the interests of mankind demand that in
such a time, social etiquette should "no longer keep man at a distance from man," nor "impose its flimsy fancies between the free
communication of intellect." [63]

"I am willing to become a scholar—nay, a pupil. My humility and confidence, where I am conscious that I am not imposed upon, and where I perceive talents and powers so certainly and undoubtedly superior, is unfeigned and complete." *Political Justice* had convinced Shelley that he had duties to perform in the world, and so he promptly sent off his little tract, *The Necessity of Atheism*, to leading ecclesiastics in the Church of England, and informed the less-active Godwin of his plan to visit Ireland, quite alone, to "forward as much as he can the Catholic Emancipation." This was the individualism of a romantic age. Somewhat untactfully, the young poet mentioned that he had felt the urge to be a disciple before: "Southey the poet, whose principles were pure and elevated once, is now the paid champion of every abuse and absurdity. I have had much conversation with him: he says, 'you will think as I do when you are old.' I do not feel the least disposition to be Mr. Southey's proselyte." [64]

On October 4 of the same year (1812), the Shelleys dined with Godwin in London and the families met almost daily for six weeks. Two years later, in the summer, Shelley met Mary Godwin again, and found her an attractive young woman of nearly seventeen. It was May 18 when he arrived; Mary disliked her stepmother and longed for the great world; Shelley was sure he was in love. On July 14, Harriet Shelley arrived in London, and Godwin tried earnestly to reconcile husband and wife. Fourteen days later, July 28, Mary and Jane Clairmont left home early in the morning, joined Shelley, took the public post to Dover, crossed the Channel in an open boat during a violent storm, and arrived in Calais. On the second day in France, their landlord brought the message that "a fat lady had arrived who said that I had run away with her daughter." But Mrs. Godwin's persuasions were of no avail, and she returned to London alone. At about the same time, young William Godwin ran away from home and could not be located for two days.[65]

After the Shelleys and Miss Clairmont returned to England, the latter was occasionally permitted to visit the Skinner Street residence of the Godwins. In March of 1816, when the Shelleys were visiting at Binfield, Godwin visited nearby Bracknell and walked over to see his daughter. From that time on there was a more friendly relationship between the families. How could the "master" have resented the action of a "pupil" in such clear accordance with the teachings of both William Godwin and Mary Wollstone-craft? In a letter addressed to Mr. John Taylor, and post-dated August 27, 1814, Godwin admits that Shelley told him of his love, shared his plans, and asked his consent on Sunday, June 26.[66] From this distance we can only guess at the turmoil of the philos-opher-father. He who was a thinker had won a disciple who was a doer. The feelings of the father about his daughter may not have matched the deliberations of the philosopher. Perhaps he consid-ered that Shelley's status as husband and father of two children disqualified him from the freedom of falling in love.

At any rate, Godwin wrote letters of impassioned accusation, but they soon gave way to petitions for financial assistance, and in March of 1816, Shelley wrote:

I confess that I do not understand how the pecuniary engagements subsisting between us in any degree impose restrictions on your con-duct towards me. . . . In my judgment neither I nor your daughter nor her offspring ought to receive the treatment which we encounter on every side. It has perpetually appeared to me to have been your especial duty to see that, so far as mankind value your good opinion, we were dealt justly by, and that a young family innocent and benev-olent and united should not be confounded with prostitutes and se-ducers. My astonishment, and I will confess—when I have been treated with harshness and cruelty by you—my indignation, has been extreme, that, knowing as you do my nature, any considerations should have pre-vailed on you to have been thus harsh and cruel. I lamented also over my ruined hopes of all that your genius once taught me to expect from your virtue, when I found that for yourself, your family, your creditors, you would submit to that communication with me, which you once re-jected and abhorred, and which no pity for my poverty or sufferings, assumed willingly for you, could avail to extort.[67]

In May, 1816, just before leaving England, Shelley wrote a sadly serene farewell:

I leave England, I know not, perhaps for ever. . . . I respect you, I think well of you, better perhaps than of any other person whom Eng-land contains. You were the philosopher who first awakened my under-standing. It is unfortunate for me that the part of your character which is least excellent should have been met by convictions of what was right to do. But I have been too indignant; I have been unjust to you; forgive me; burn those letters which contain the records of my violence, and believe that however what you call fame and honour separate us, I shall always feel toward you as the most affectionate of friends.[68]

On October 11, Fanny Godwin, on her way to South Wales to visit her aunts Everina Wollstonecraft and Mrs. Bishop, committed suicide by taking laudanum in the Mackworth Arms Inn at Swansea. On Saturday, November 9, Harriet Shelley drowned herself in the Serpentine, Kensington Gardens, London, and the body was not found until December 10. The immediate cause of her depression was the self-righteous cruelty of her sister who would not allow Harriet to come to the bedside of their dying father. On Monday, December 30, Percy Bysshe Shelley married Mary Wollstonecraft Godwin at St. Mildred's Church, Bread Street, London, with William and Mary Jane Godwin present.[69]

Shelley always considered his elopement with Mary as the mere practice of principles both her father and mother held and taught. And later critics and historians have generally sustained Shelley's side of the argument. However, this is to be insensitive to the strains and changes in Godwin's life and faith. He was being castigated as a moral monster. His beautifully restrained memoir of his wife was read as scatological literature. He made a slender living by writing books for children—anonymously, because his own name was anathema. At this moment his step-daughter Claire ran off to be Byron's mistress and his daughter Mary went away with a man already married and the father of children—a man who knew her father disapproved of the match. Because of the double scandal, his step-daughter Fanny could not be employed in her aunts' school in Ireland—perhaps her one chance to rid her beloved step-father of her support. In shock and despair Fanny Imlay committed suicide—and one wonders what kept Godwin from joining her in the same sad solution. And even after her death, Godwin dared not claim the body of this loved one for fear the newspapers might connect his name with the unfortunate suicide and bring about his utter ruin. But, as J. Middleton Murry has lamented, "the tradition of cheap, vulgar, and heartless criticism of William Godwin still endures; it will be a long while yet before it is extirpated." [70]

[74]

The rumor still circulates that Godwin sold his own daughter to Shelley in order to obtain perpetual financial aid. Certainly it seemed on the surface that he had condemned Shelley for putting into practice his own theories. But it must be borne in mind that, in the second edition of the *Memoir*, published in 1798, a significant shift of attitude is recorded; in it marriage is ranked among those customs and institutions with which, even though we might disapprove of them as individuals, "an accurate morality will direct us to comply." [71]

By 1817 the relations between the Shelleys and the Godwins seemed somewhat less strained. Shelley writes in March: "It was spring when I wrote to you, and winter when your answer arrived. But the frost is very transitory; every bud is ready to burst into leaf. The oak and the chestnut, the latest and the earliest parents of foliage, would afford you a still subtler sub-division, which would enable you to defer the visit, from which we expect so much delight, for six weeks." Several letters follow concerning Godwin's critical estimates of Shelley's *Laon and Cythna* (1818). After this date, the letters grow less frequent. One from Shelley in August, 1820, uses a cool and distant "sir" instead of "my dear Godwin" in refusing him financial assistance. The pupil instructs the schoolmaster that "it is an additional consolation to me to have been shown that I ought not." Within a few years he has given Godwin "a considerable fortune." But even in this letter, and to the very end, one can sense the old boyish respect for the great philosophical mind as an attitude that manages to survive the financial depredations and the niggling needs of Godwin's household. [72] And once when Godwin's fortunes were at one of their frequent nadirs, Mary Shelley promptly sent a novel in manuscript, *Valperga*, and generously begged her father to publish it and keep the proceeds to carry him through his financial embarrassments. After some reluctance, Godwin accepted her insistent offer, revised the work to fit his own estimate of the popular taste, and published it. [73]

In 1830 a new acquaintance was made, the last of the long series of younger friends. Edward Bulwer, later Lord Lytton, while a student at Cambridge, was introduced to Godwin by Lady Caroline Lamb. The general correspondence between the older mentor and the enthusiastic youth follows the usual pattern, but one remarkable literary consequence of the friendship emerges. Godwin, who had long intended to write a romance on the story of Eugene Aram (a schoolmaster who had been executed for murder in 1759), had drawn up a series of notes and a prospectus on the subject. Although it is without date, the paper, style of writing, the package in which it was found, all point to the period 1828-30. Just as it is clear that Bulwer-Lytton's early literary style is an intellectual descendent of Godwin's *Caleb Williams* and *St. Leon,* so it is at least worthy of a conjecture that the older writer decided he could never finish the projected work and turned over his notes to his young, vigorous friend. At any rate, Edward Bulwer-Lytton published a novel in 1832 entitled *Eugene Aram. A Tale.*[74] Even Godwin's characteristic attitude toward the criminal is reflected in the social conditions that "force" Aram to consent to the murder.

V *Essayist*

It is not easy to separate Godwin the essayist from the defender and the pamphleteer. The pamphlets and legal briefs that have already been examined were related in some particular to his friends and the political struggles of his day. The prose writing presented in this section of this chapter is of a more general and philosophical type. *The Enquirer: Reflections on Education, Manners, and Literature, in a Series of Essays* was published by William Godwin in 1797, and again in 1823. *The Enquirer* was stylistically indebted to Godwin's journalistic contributions to *The Political Herald* and the *New Annual Register.* The systematic style of *Political Justice,* with its basic postulates and the deductions derived from them, is abandoned, as well as the intense narrative style and the highly rhetorical dialogue style of *Caleb Williams.* The manner of the personal essay of Joseph Addison and Richard Steele is adopted in *The Enquirer;* and a series of informal discussions on serious topics, but in discursive and conversational tone, is produced. Each topic is discussed quite independently; the only division in thought is represented by Part I on personal topics: "Awakening the Mind," "Utility of Talents," "Sources of Genius," "An Early Taste for Reading," etc.; and Part II on public issues, such as "Riches and Poverty," "Servants," "Trades and Professions," "Posthumous Fame," "Age of Queen

Anne," and "Age of George the Second." Part II is also notable for a lengthy discussion of English style.

This deliberate choice of a style quite different from his published books, but similar to his journalistic work, creates easy and persuasive reading but seldom lifts the reader by any particular distinction of language. Yet there are the characteristic pithy Godwin comments that are entirely consistent as well as unique. Concerning education, he writes, "A young person should be educated as if he were one day to become a man." [75] In the period of his public decline, he found many opportunities in the writing and editing of children's books to implement this conviction. Just as in *Political Justice* he saw law arising out of the protection of property rights, a large group of essays is devoted to the problems created by the established system of property: wealth and poverty, benefactors and beggars, professions and trades. The section on self-denial avoids the extremes of asceticism and indulgence and stresses the early Classical virtues of moderation and temperance as against the luxury and licentiousness of the Augustan period with which the men of the eighteenth century were so fond of identifying themselves. In the three essays on personal reputation, he steers cautiously between iconoclasm and the desire for popularity, pointing out the uses of public approval, but not less its limits and vulgarity.

The second essay in Part II, "Of Avarice and Profusion," advocates the Godwinian ideal of a society of "cultivated equality." Far more significant than any one thing Godwin says in the essay is its remarkable influence. The Reverend Thomas Robert Malthus read the essay and was challenged to write in reply his *Essay on Population*, published the following year. In objection to the perfectionism and utopian egalitarianism of such writers as William Godwin and Marie Antoine, Marquis de Condorcet, Malthus developed the thesis that, while subsistence increases only arithmetically, population tends to increase geometrically; thus population is constantly outstripping the available food supply. Nor did the creative power of Godwin's essay end there; Charles Darwin, in the nineteenth century, expressed his indebtedness to Malthus' treatise for his theory of the struggle for survival as applied to biological species.

The final seven essays in *The Enquirer* (Part II, Section 31) are on the topic of English literary style. With charmingly naïve self-esteem, Godwin states that "the English language was never in so high a state of purity and perfection, as in the present reign of King George the Third." [76] Considering his critical judgments on most of the other institutions of the period, it seems odd that he finds this style so excellent, but perhaps it is the delusion of any era that it represents a quintessence of the best that has gone before. Godwin's supporting evidence is also decidedly odd for so logical a mind. He quotes examples of faulty prose from previous ages, thus condemning them; but he never attempts to match these bad examples with good examples from his own time. His demand for "clearness, propriety and compression" in prose style can scarcely be improved upon. But this critical standard blinds him to the baroque glories of Richard Hooker's *Ecclesiastical Polity*, which by application of the rule, seems "somewhat loitering and tedious." In the field of poetry, he considered Milton, Dryden, Butler, and Otway to have written in "the golden age of English poetry." This is scarcely a surprising conclusion, but it is interesting to note that his autobiographical fragment states that in two years, 1799-1800, he abandoned his previous literary canons and enthusiastically rated Elizabethan literature in first place.

In 1809, when public opinion had turned against Godwin— ". . . there are numbers of men who overflow with gall and prejudice against me (God bless them!)" [77]—he wrote the one hundred and nineteen page *Essay on Sepulchres: or a Proposal for Erecting Some Memorial of the Illustrious Dead in All Ages on the Spot Where Their Remains have been Interred.*[78] Like Sir Thomas Browne, he wished "to live in intercourse with the Illustrious Dead of all Ages"; but, unlike him, he believed in the power of visible memorials to immortalize a memory.

In his Preface he gives us a hint of his manner of composition: "To write with fervour, and to revise at leisure." [79] The formula suggests that the fervor of the novels and the marmoreal coldness of the essays are equally and perhaps consecutively his own. The Preface closes with an idea which is reinforced by Godwin's belief that all ideas and impressions come to a man through outer sensations; he cannot accept the creed of Bishop Berkeley that "the body . . . the vehicle through which the knowledge of these thoughts and virtues was conveyed to me, was nothing." [80] Thus the sensational realist replies to the absolute idealist. The perfectibility of man is the basis of his contention that death is the calamitous reason "the world forever is, and in some degree for ever must be, in its infancy." [81] If man is capable of perpetual improvement, death cuts off growth; and the man who has grown mightily is superseded by the infant who has no development at all.

The Reverend Thomas Robert Malthus published his treatise on population anonymously in 1798. However, no particular secret was made of the authorship, and the fourth edition, published five years later, carried the author's name. Mr. Malthus was Fellow of Jesus College, Cambridge, and from 1804 until his death in 1831, Professor of History and Political Economics at Haileybury College. In a letter to William Godwin, dated August 20, 1798, Malthus stated as the main contention of his treatise that assistance should be refused to poverty for the purpose of preventing overpopulation, which he considered to be the main cause of the evils apparent in human life, rather than Godwin's contention that government is that evil. [82]

Godwin wrote a reply to Malthus, *Of Population,* in 1820. "I hailed the attack of Mr. Malthus. I believed that the *Essay on Population,* like other erroneous and exaggerated representations of things, would soon find its own level . . . the theory of this writter flattered the vices and corruption of the rich and the great, and the eager patronage it might very naturally be expected to gain from them." [83] Godwin attacks the central principle of Malthus' work, that population increases geometrically whereas subsistence increases only arithmetically, and that, therefore, unless population is, in some manner kept down, the earth will be entirely cultivated and there will be no place left to plant food. Godwin lists Malthus' eleven checks on population: unwholesome occupations, severe labor, exposure to the season, extreme poverty, bad nursing of children, great towns, excesses of all kinds, common diseases and epidemics, wars, plague, famine. He points out in the Preface that Malthus' thesis would be most grateful news to industrialists and to employers and wealthy persons generally, for it would give scientific and sociological sanction to what their selfishness made them want to do anyway. Malthus' conclusion was that, if a Utopia embodying the principles of Godwin's *Political Justice* were to be established, population growth would destroy it within thirty years.

Godwin's answer is organized as a dialogue debate, with a statement by Malthus, including his reasons for the statement, followed by rebuttal and reasons from Godwin. Malthus thus argues that "population, when unchecked, goes on doubling itself every twenty-five years, or increases in a geometrical ratio . . . [as] in the northern states of America, the population has been found so to double itself for above a century and a half successively" (Book I, Introduction). Godwin replies: "I think I shall be able to make out that the power of increase in the numbers of the human species is extremely small." He then proceeds to point out that the population of the ancient world was at least as large as at the present day. (At this point, Godwin was undoubtedly misled by literal acceptance of the numerology of ancient manuscripts and critical evaluation of current statistics.) Because of his concern for overpopulation, Malthus warns men of the evils of marriage (Book I, Section xiii). And the political philosopher who had called marriage the worst form of monopoly proceeds to quote ancient and modern authors on the blessings of marriage and parenthood. Malthus advises the abolition of poor-laws—"disclaim the right of the poor to support," for "every man has a right to do what he will with his own" (Book II, Section iii). Godwin counters by claiming that the problem is not to keep the population down but to bring subsistence up, for wherever one person now lives, the earth is capable of supporting fifteen (V, ii). It is government ("positive institutions") that lowers the level of subsistence by its abuses of the farmer. Godwin adds the example of Mr. Coke's model Norfolk estate, and he suggests that the seas represent a great, relatively untouched source of subsistence. At the close of the argument, Godwin rhetorically throws his hands into the air as he builds the Malthusian syllogism: Guard against hunger and famine by encouraging vice and misery, all for the well-being of society! (VI, i).

Godwin had assumed that a thesis such as Malthus' would fall by its own dreadful weight. But it did not fall, and so after an interval of twenty-two years, he set himself to the systematic and ambitious task of compiling such a work that the world would be finally and forever rid of the "accursed apology in favour of vice and misery, of hard-heartedness and oppression." [84] But *Of Population* (1820) was too late; Godwin's reputation was too diminished, and the personal interest of the reigning classes too strong. The upshot was that the book which was to rid the world of a pestilent sanction for social abuses failed even to realize enough to pay for its printing.

William Godwin often described his mind as "constitutionally meditative" and so it was suitable that the fruit of his meditations appear under the title *Thoughts on Man, His Nature, Productions, and Discoveries, Interspersed with Some Particulars Respecting the Author,* in 1831, just five years before his death. Toward the end of his life, as at the beginning of his literary career, his faith in the perfectibility of man never faltered. In the Preface to these collected essays, he states once again his humanistic credo:

I know many men who are misanthropes, and profess to look down with disdain on their species. My creed is of an opposite character. All that we observe that is best and most excellent in the intellectual world, is man: and it is easy to perceive in many cases, that the believer in mysteries does little more, than draw up his deity in the choicest of human attributes and qualifications. I have lived among, and I feel an ardent interest in and love for, my brethren of mankind. This sentiment, which I regard with complacency in my own breast, I would gladly cherish in others. In such a cause I am well pleased to enroll myself a missionary. [85]

The essay titles run much the same gamut as the table of contents of *The Enquirer:* "Of Body and Mind," "Of the Distribution of Talents," "Of Intellectual Abortion," "Of the Durability of Human Achievements and Productions," "Of the Rebelliousness of Man," "Of Human Innocence," "Of the Duration of Human Life," "Of Human Vegetation," "Of Leisure," "Of Imitation and Invention," "Of Self-Love and Benevolence," "Of the Liberty of Human Actions," "Of Belief," "Of Youth and Age," "Of Love and Friendship," "Of Frankness and Reserve," "Of Ballot," "Of Diffidence," "Of Self-Complacency," "Of Phrenology," "Of Astronomy," "Of the Material Universe," "Of Human Virtue." Perhaps one can note the dominant interests of old age in more of the titles than in those of the earler collections, but style and philosophic groundwork remain the same. As the Preface introduced the motif, the final essay on human virtue repeats it: "Let us then pay to human virtue the honour that is justly its due!" [86]

At his death Godwin left a series of essays on religious subjects entitled *The Genius of Christianity Unveiled.* He evidently expected Mary Shelley to revise and publish the manuscript immediately, for in a letter addressed to her, dated only a few days before his death, he says: "I leave behind me a manuscript in a considerable state of forwardness for the press, entitled, 'The Genius of Christianity Unveiled: in a Series of Essays.'" The letter concludes with these earnest words: "I am most unwilling that this, the concluding work of a long life, and written, as I believe, in the full maturity of my understanding, should be consigned to oblivion." [87] Whatever may have weighed more heavily than these solemn words, Mrs. Shelley did not publish them, but they were finally published by her literary representatives, as *Essays Never Before Published* in 1873.

The preliminary essay on "the exoteric and esoteric in philosophy and theology" states that Egyptians, Pythagoreans, Hindoos, and Druids have been of the opinion that "there is one set of doctrines that it is convenient should be recommended to and imposed upon the vulgar, and another that should be communicated only to such as were found unquestionably worthy of that favour and distinction." Thus, by analogy, Godwin suggests that in his own time, the upper hierarchy of the clergy, although they may believe little that is recited in the liturgy of public worship, must make a public profession of that non-existent belief in order to satisfy the lower ranks of the lay religious. It outrages Godwin's conviction of the importance of sincerity in human relationships that "the man who professes infidelity among his confidential associates is the very person who is the most systematical in enforcing orthodoxy upon his inferiors."

The essays themselves include such topics as a state of future retribution, the present life of man considered as a state of probation for a future world, contrition, the death of Jesus considered as an atonement for sin, Providence, what one must do to be saved, faith and works, the character of Jesus, the history and effects of the Christian religion, liberty, the mixed character of Christianity—its horrors and its graces, the character of God as described in the Scriptures, the idea of an intelligent Creator, Nature, and Miracles. With a noble expression of eighteenth-century Stoicism, he concludes: "To be independent and erect is essential to the perfect man. To stand in awe of neither matter nor spirit. To fear (for fear we must) those things which in the world of realities we may encounter, and which may subdue us. But to fear nothing unnecessarily, and with superstition. And, *si fractus illabatur orbis,* to witness the ruin with a calm and composed frame of spirit." And again Godwin states the old, steadfast theme of the possibilities of man if only he can free himself from those positive institutions that cripple his growth: "We know not what we might have been. But surely we should have been greater than we are, but for this disadvantage. It is as if we took some minute poison with everything that was intended to nourish us . . . insensibly change us, from giants of mind, which we might have been, into a people of dwarfs." [88]

CHAPTER 4

Novels and Plays

Mr. Godwin, during his lifetime, has secured to himself the triumphs and the mortifications of an extreme notoriety and of a sort of posthumous fame . . . he is to all ordinary intents and purposes dead and buried; but the author of *Political Justice* and of *Caleb Williams* can never die, his name is an abstraction in letters, his works are standard in the history of intellect. He is thought of now like any eminent writer a hundred-and-fifty years ago, or just as he will be a hundred-and-fifty years hence. He knows this, and smiles in silent mockery of himself. . . .

> WILLIAM HAZLITT, "Contemporary Portraits," *The Spirit of the Age*, 1825

I *The Novel*

ONE temptation of a writer on Godwin is to portray a hideous blood-sucker who clung to the circle of Shelley and his friends. Another is to make him merely the husband of Mary Wollstonecraft. A third temptation is to discuss *Political Justice* in great detail, examine *Caleb Williams* as a strange literary hybrid, and taper off with a dying fall on *St. Leon*. A treatment such as the third ignores the preacher and pamphleteer, the historian and biographer, the educator and the novelist, and damns the dramatist by complete silence. But the study of the novels and the dramas advances the thought of William Godwin from rigid rationalism, which modern critics find forbidding, to persuasive idealism, which had so profound an influence on his contemporaries. Quite deliberately, the political philosopher wrote *Caleb Williams* to clothe ideas in the living flesh of fiction.

What is now [May 12, 1794] presented to the public, is no refined and abstract speculation: it is a study and delineation of things passing in the moral world. It is but of late that the inestimable importance of political principles has been adequately apprehended. It is now known to philosophers, that the spirit and character of the government intrudes itself into every rank of society. But this is a truth, highly worthy to be communicated, to persons, whom books of philosophy and science are never likely to reach. Accordingly it was proposed, in the invention of the following work, to comprehend, as far as the progressive nature of a single story would allow, a general review of the modes of domestic and unrecorded despotism, by which man becomes the destroyer of man.[1]

Damon and Delia, Italian Letters, *1783;* Imogen, *1784*

Godwin noted in his Journal that, after he wrote *The History of the Life of William Pitt, Earl of Chatham* in 1783, his principal employment was writing articles at two guineas a sheet for the *English Review,* published by Murray in Fleet Street. This was a very busy time: "In the latter end of 1783 I wrote in ten days a novel entitled *Damon and Delia,* for which Hookham gave me five guineas, and a novel in three weeks called *Italian Letters,* purchased by Robinson for twenty guineas, and in the first four months of 1784 a novel called *Imogen, a Pastoral Romance,* for which Lane gave me ten pounds." [2] Perhaps fortunately, these rapidly-written manuscripts, paid for by the pound, have become mere notations in a diary.

Things As They Are, or the Adventures of Caleb Williams, *1794*

In 1794, Godwin wrote a doctrinaire novel, *Caleb Williams,* which, along with *Political Justice,* seemed to William Hazlitt to guarantee undying fame to its author. During the year of composition, Godwin said to himself a thousand times, "I will write a tale, that shall constitute an epoch in the mind of the reader, that no one, after he has read it, shall ever be exactly the same man that he was before." In describing the genesis of the plot, he mentions an old book, *The Adventures of Mademoiselle de St. Phale,* "a French Protestant in the times of the fiercest persecution of the Huguenots, who fled through France in the utmost terror, in the midst of eternal alarms and hair-breadth escapes, having her quarters perpetually beaten up, and by scarcely any chance finding a moment's interval of security."

He also browsed through the pages of a vast volume, *God's Revenge against Murder,* in which "the beam of the eye of Omniscience was represented as perpetually pursuing the guilty, and laying open the most hidden retreats to the light of day." He also mentions the *Newgate Calendar,* the *Lives of the Pirates,* and any assorted fiction that happened to come to hand, providing it was "written with energy." In a somewhat ghoulish image he describes the authors of these works, and himself, as "all of us engaged in exploring the entrails of mind and motive." He also related the story of Caleb Williams and the tale of Bluebeard: "Falkland was my Bluebeard, who had perpetrated atrocious crimes, which if discovered, he might expect to have all the world roused to revenge against him. Caleb Williams was the wife, who in spite of warning, persisted in his attempts to discover the forbidden secret, and, when he had succeeded, struggled as fruitlessly to escape the consequences, as the wife of Bluebeard in washing the key of the ensanguined chamber, who, as often as she cleared the stain of blood from the one side, found it showing itself with frightful distinctness on the other." [3]

The genesis of the plot, and the motto on the title page of the first edition—

> Amidst the woods the leopard knows his kind;
> The tyger preys not on the tyger brood;
> Man only is the common foe of man.—

suggest that this will be a classic study of cruel, unrelenting human pursuit. The novel became such a common byword that Byron, in one of his quarrels with Lady Byron, threatened to persecute her even as Falkland had persecuted Caleb.[4] A comparison of William Godwin's *Caleb Williams* with Mary Shelley's *Frankenstein* shows the clear resemblance of the "creature" of a gifted man turning upon his "creator" and pursuing him to his death.

The anonymous author of the *Memoirs of William Godwin* testifies that "All that might have offended, as hard and republican in his larger work [*Political Justice*], was obliterated by the splendour and noble beauty of the character of Falkland . . . He tells a tale of injustice and oppression, and every feeling of indignant resistance stirs within us . . . The principal object of his study and contemplation is man the enemy of man." [5] Ferdinando Falkland, nurtured on romance and chivalry, the "fool of honour and of fame," returns to his country estate. Here he finds a neighboring squire, Barnabas Tyrrel, admired for his physical strength and political power, and, because of his social standing, permitted to perform acts of the most irresponsible tyranny. Tyrrel first protects a small freeholder, Hawkins, and then persecutes him bitterly for his sturdy refusal to place his beloved only son in service. He first dotes on his plain but sprightly cousin Emily Melville; but, when she is rescued from a fire by Falkland, he determines to marry her to a lout in revenge for her praise of her rescuer. Emily is rescued from a forced marriage by Falkland's intervention, but she dies of the mental, emotional, and physical exertions involved. Falkland, in horror, attempts to ostracize Tyrrel, but is publicly beaten and kicked. This dishonor he avenges by stabbing Tyrrel in the darkness outside the hall they had just left. The murder is blamed on Hawkins, who clearly has an adequate motive. He and his son are executed for the crime, and Falkland's greater need for public esteem than for private honor keeps him silent. This, presumably, is the state of "Things As They Are"—a world in which the rich and well-born can exercise any kind of tyranny and violence, except against a member of their own economic class.

In a curious way, the story seems closed before Caleb even enters the narrative. The orphaned, sixteen-year-old boy is hired benevolently by Falkland as secretary and librarian. If Falkland is the fool of honor, Williams is mastered by an obsessive curiosity. He must discover what so distresses his master, what he keeps in an old trunk, what has turned the popular and gifted social personality into a melancholy recluse. Loving his master, he yet with unholy zeal unmasks his crime; and then, in one of the strangest miscarriages of justice, the criminal relentlessly pursues and persecutes his innocent discoverer. "He [Godwin] gets up, goes abroad into 'the throng miscalled society,' sees only its errors and its vices, its knaves and its dupes; and writes as if little or nothing else was in existence." [6]

At last the quarry turns and appeals for vindication to the very justice he already knows is entirely on the side of his guilty foe.

The author has shown clearly, that at least in the life of Caleb Williams, the corrupt and corrupting "spirit and character of the government intrudes itself into every rank of society." [7] By the appeal of his hero to law, that instrument of "domestic and unrecorded despotism," he is sure to invoke the completion of the sentence—"by which man becomes the destroyer of man." Caleb is vindicated and his master confesses, "I see too late the greatness and elevation of your mind." Falkland is guilty; but, in his death, Caleb admits, "I have been his murderer . . . he . . . has fallen a victim, life and fame, to my precipitation! It would have been merciful in comparison if I had planted a dagger in his heart . . . I endure the penalty of my crime." [8] In consistency with the Godwinian philosophy of the influence of environment, the murderer ends the tale exonerated:

Falkland! thou enteredst upon thy career with the purest and most laudable intentions. But thou imbibedst the poison of chivalry with thy earliest youth; and the base and low-minded envy that met thee on thy return to thy native seats, operated with this poison to hurry thee into madness. Soon, too soon, by this fatal coincidence, were the blooming hopes of thy youth blasted for ever! From that moment thou only continuedst to live to the phantom of departed honour. From that moment thy benevolence was, in great part, turned into rankling jealousy and inexorable precaution. Year after year didst thou spend in this miserable project of imposture; and only at last continuedst to live, long enough to see, by my misjudging and abhorred intervention, thy closing hope disappointed, and thy death accompanied with the foulest disgrace! [9]

In other words, in accord with Godwinian principles, Falkland began life with a completely clean slate. He was falsely educated in the virtues and traditions of romance and chivalry. When he returned to his country estate, by the purest coincidence he met a base and low-minded antagonist. Thus the trap was both baited and set from without. What should have blossomed as benevolence, withered as jealousy and caution. Instead of frank sincerity, he spent his days in imposture. His disgraceful end came, not as the natural culmination of his own deeds and attitudes, but by the misjudgment and intervention of someone else (Caleb Williams) from the outside.

Thus Falkland, representing the "man of taste" in Godwin's

[88]

hierarchy of human values, was clearly meant by nature to grad-uate into "man of universal benevolence." But he is felled by mistaken education in a chivalric ideal of honor and by coinci-dentally meeting the three persons—Tyrrel, Hawkins, and Wil-liams—most perfectly able to act upon that weakness. And so the criminal deserves sympathy and the innocent accuser odium, for "If he had been criminal, that is owing to circumstances; the same qualities under other circumstances would have been, or rather were, sublimely beneficent." [10]

It was David Hartley's hierarchy of pleasures that became God-win's scale of the four stages of happiness: uncultivated peasant, man of wealth and fashion, man of taste, man of benevolence.[11] Tyrrel and Falkland represent not only two stages in the scale of human development (wealth and taste), but also the principle of despotism (Tyrrel) versus the spirit of monarchy (Falkland). When Godwin shows that Falkland is as much the victim of honor as Caleb is the victim of obsessive curiosity, he moves his critique of Charles, Baron de Montesquieu's ideal of honor, from argument to demonstration. Honor was incapable of creating har-monious social relationships; it was equally incapable of being the guiding principle of an individual life.[12]

It is clear that the idyllic picture of the simple life in Wales, the sympathy for and exoneration of a triple murderer, the emphasis upon man as victim of circumstance rather than maker of destiny, the strong appeal to humanitarianism, all build up to emotional-ism, or even sentimentality, that goes far beyond the measured aphorisms of *Political Justice;* and, to a large degree, these quali-ties explain the marked influence Godwin's novel had on his con-temporaries, particularly on responsive youth.[13] The reference to sentimentalism deserves more amplification than the account thus far has given. Falkland performs the "sentimental rescue" by sav-ing Emily from fire; Caleb describes Raymond, the robber chief, as magnamimous and noble; the pathos of Emily's death is matched by the death-bed rhetoric of Falkland. In *Caleb Wil-liams,* Godwin begins to walk on a path that will take him far from legalism and, in subsequent works, close to the novel of sen-timent.

The anonymous writer of the *Memoirs* attributes to Godwin the talent of telling a tale "like one who remembers, not invents. Thus his story becomes not the relation of a looker-on, however acute and powerful, but is 'compact' of words hot from the burnt and branded heart of the miserable sufferer." [14] The political metaphysician turned writer of popular romance was more depressed than elated when he finished the work which was to be acclaimed his best novel and one of the classic novels of obsessive curiosity and relentless pursuit: "When I had done all, what had I done? Written a book to amuse boys and girls in their vacant hours, a story to be hastily gobbled up by them, swallowed in a pusillanimous and unanimated mood, without chewing and digestion." His friend Joseph Gerald told him, doubtless as the highest of compliments, that having started Volume One late in the evening, he was unable to close his eyes in sleep until he had read through all three volumes. What must have been his astonishment to hear the disgruntled author mutter, "Thus, what had cost me twelve months' labour, ceaseless heart-aches and industry, now sinking in despair, and now roused and sustained in unusual energy, he went over in a few hours, shut the book, laid himself on his pillow, slept and was refreshed, and cried, 'To-morrow to fresh woods and pastures new.'" [15]

St. Leon, *1799*

In 1799, William Godwin published *St. Leon: A Tale of the Sixteenth Century,* with the warning motto from Congreve: "Ferdinand Mendez Pinto was but a type of thee, thou liar of the first magnitude." The Advertisement afforded the author an opportunity to describe the process that led from *Caleb Williams* to *St. Leon:*

In 1794 I produced the novel of *Caleb Williams.* I believed myself fortunate in the selection I had made of the ground-plot of that work. An atrocious crime committed by a man previously of the most exemplary habits, the annoyance he suffers from the immeasurable and ever-wakeful curiosity of a raw youth who is placed about his person, the state of doubt in which the reader might for a time be as to the truth of the charges, and the consequences growing out of these causes, seemed to me to afford scope for a narrative of no common interest.

Now, with a successful first novel behind him, the second is begun. "At length, after having passed some years in a state of diffidence and irresolution, I ventured on the task. It struck me that if I could 'mix human feelings and passions with incredible situations,' I might thus attain a sort of novelty that would conciliate the patience, at least, even of some of the severest judges. To this way of thinking St. Leon was indebted for a 'local habitation, and a name.'" [16] By an odd coincidence, the mixture of ordinary life with the incredible sounds strikingly like the Preface to the *Lyrical Ballads* of the year before and also like the fourteenth chapter of the *Biographia Literaria* in which Wordsworth was set the task of giving "the charm of novelty to things of every day," and Coleridge the essentially more Romantic task of winning that "willing suspension of unbelief" by which the unusual may be accepted as the usual.[17]

With his customary exemplary frankness in admitting sources, Godwin refers to a statement from Dr. John Campbel's translation of Johann Heinrich Cohausen's *Hermippus Redivivus,* which describes a Signor Gualdi, visitor to Venice in 1687, whose small collection of fine paintings contained his portrait painted by Titian more than one hundred and thirty years before. "It is well known that the philosopher's stone, the art of transmuting metals into gold, and the *elixir vitae,* which was to restore youth, and make him that possessed it immortal; formed a principal object of the studies of the curious for centuries. Many stories, beside this of Signor Gualdi, have been told, of persons who were supposed to be in possession of these wonderful secrets, in search of which hundreds of unfortunate adventurers wasted their fortunes and their lives." [18]

But, in distinguishing literary sources, we must not neglect the importance of Godwin's union with Mary Wollstonecraft in the interval between the publication of *Caleb Williams* and *St. Leon.* The character of Marguerite, in the latter novel, is clearly indebted to the personality of Mary, and a striking change may be noted in the doctrine expressed in *Political Justice* that the private affections are the main blocks that stand in the way of the achievement of universal benevolence. *St. Leon* marks a long step forward in Godwin's recognition of the importance of emotion as a motive for conduct and as a basis of relationship. The novel expresses his hard-won conviction that the experience of family affection is essential to the complete development of the individual personality, and can, in its turn, act as a stepping stone toward universal benevolence. "I have learned to value my domestic blessings as I ought." [19]

In the novel, St. Leon is reared by his mother and, like Falkland, early imbibes the ideals of chivalry and honor. As a Count of St. Leon, at the age of fifteen, he is present at the meeting of Francis I and Henry VIII at Ardes in June, 1520. When he is twenty, he marries the nineteen-year-old Marguerite de Danville, and they are blessed with children: Charles, Julia, Louise, and Marguerite. When Charles is nine, his father takes him to Paris to enter school; but he remains himself to live splendidly and gamble until he is beggared at the gaming tables. Marguerite makes up his debts with her estate and the inheritance of their children. The impoverished family lives in patriarchal simplicity in Switzerland until a storm destroys their dwelling. At Marspurg, Reginald St. Leon is cheated out of the remainder of his estate and takes a job as assistant gardener. With a gift of money from a servant, Bernardin, Reginald returns to Soleure and manages to obtain financial redress from the Council.

At the beginning of Volume II, Reginald is visited by Signor Francesca Zampieri of Venice, who is in flight from the police. Protected by St. Leon, and close to death, he gives him the secret of the philosopher's stone with its power to transmute base metal into gold and to grant eternal life. The sudden and suspicious wealth of his father makes Charles leave his family, leads the townspeople to accuse Reginald of the stranger's death, and brings his wife to invalidism. Volume III moves the family to Pisa, where a brief interval for Reginald as good father and husband is climaxed by Marguerite's delivery of a dead child and her own subsequent death. The widower purchases the St. Leon ancestral estates, settles his daughters there with a companion, and departs—for their protection. He is imprisoned by the Holy Inquisition for twelve years, but escapes in the crowd assembled for his *auto-da-fé*. His tribulations have made him appear eighty at the age of fifty-four, but the elixir of life restores him to the appearance and vigor of twenty.

In Volume IV Reginald moves to Hungary, which, in 1560, was torn between Solyman the Turk and Charles of Austria. He determines to rescue a whole nation from poverty and fear through his great powers. Initially praised, he is finally universally execrated, so that he fears for his life. He turns to a local strong man, Bethlem Gabor, who at first is attracted to him, but later despises him for his unwillingness to seek revenge. The misanthropic Gabor, learning his secret, locks Reginald in his dungeons, from which he is rescued by his own son Charles, now a renowned knight under the banner of Austria. Reginald becomes his son's best friend and arranges for his marriage to Pandora, niece of the Palatine of Hungary. After various misunderstandings, in which Charles becomes jealous of his own father, discovers that he is an alchemist, and appoints a time and place for a duel, all is cleared up; and the father can exclaim:

"I was the hero's father.—but no! I am not blinded by paternal partiality;—but no! he was indeed what I thought him, as near the climax of dignity and virtue as the frailty of our nature will admit. His virtue was at length crowned with the most enviable reward the earth has to boast,—the faithful attachment of a noble-minded and accomplished woman. I am happy to close my eventful and melancholy story with so pleasing a termination. Whatever may have been the result of my personal experience of human life, I can never recollect the fate of Charles and Pandora without confessing with exultation, that this busy and anxious world of ours yet contains something in its stores that is worth living for." [20]

St. Leon has been reared as an aristocrat and trained in the opulent display and imposture of hereditary wealth. This training was necessary for him or for any other aristocrat, in order that his false position as exalted, different, and superior to other men might be maintained. When he gambles away all the advantages wealth gives, he lives a pastoral existence with his wife and children. His wife confesses that

". . . it is, I fear, too true, that the splendour in which we lately lived has its basis in oppression; and that the superfluities of the rich are a boon extorted from the hunger and misery of the poor! Here we see a peasantry more peaceful and less oppressed than perhaps any other tract of the earth can exhibit. They are erect and independent, at once friendly and fearless. Is not this a refreshing spectacle: I now begin practically to perceive that the cultivators of the fields and the vineyards are my brethren and my sisters; and my heart bounds with joy, as I feel my relations to society multiply. How cumbrous is magnificence! The moderate man is the only free." [21]

Thus the novelist-philosopher's accents are muted through Marguerite's lips. Godwin's voice is heard again when St. Leon contemplates his family in their Swiss cottage: "What are gold and jewels and precious utensils? Mere dross and dirt. The human face and the human heart, reciprocations of kindness and love, and all the nameless sympathies of our nature, these are the only objects worth being attached to." [22]

But, when St. Leon learns the secret of alchemy and immortality from the stranger, all his slumbering aristocratic pretensions burst into life. In Hungary he assumes the roles of god, benevolent despot, and plutocratic patron; and he attempts to do for a whole nation the things only the citizens can do for themselves. The political philosopher speaks again in the defense of St. Leon's misanthropic betrayer, Bethlem Gabor. He is a misanthrope, not a philanthropist, but he must be understood, not condemned. Like Shakespeare's Macduff, his hatred is the result of his outraged affection for a wife and family slaughtered in their own castle in his absence. Because he had loved so intensely and still longed so tirelessly for his deceased family, "He never saw a festive board without an inclination to overturn it; or a father encircled with a smiling family, without feeling his soul thrill with suggestions of murder." [23]

This *rationale* is a far cry from the Satanic pose and the embodied evil of the villains of the Romantic writers. On the other hand, echoes of Goethe's Werther and pre-figurings of Byron's Manfred rebound from the scene in which Reginald rages with a storm, and hopes death will take him:

The wildness of an untamed and savage scene best accorded with the temper of my mind. I sprung from cliff to cliff among the points of the rock. I rushed down precipices that to my sobered sense appeared in a manner perpendicular, and only preserved my life, with a sort of inborn and unelective care, by catching at the roots and shrubs which occasionally broke the steepness of the descent. I hung over the tops of rocks still more fearful in their declivities, and courted the giddiness and whirl of spirit which such spectacles are accustomed to produce.

I could not resolve to die: death had too many charms to suit the self-condemnation that pursued me; I found a horrible satisfaction in determining to live, and to avenge upon myself the guilt I had incurred.[24]

St. Leon sought out the friendship of Gabor, not only because he needed protection, but also because he longed for a friend: "Man was not born to live alone. He is linked to his brethren by a thousand ties; and, when those ties are broken, he ceases from all genuine existence. Their complacence is a boon more invigorating than ambrosia; their aversion is a torment worse than that of the damned." [25] He looks back and realizes that his aristocratic pretensions limited the possibilities of friendship: "Equality is the soul of real and cordial society. A man of rank indeed does not live upon equal terms with the whole of his species; but his heart also can exult, for he has his equals." [26]

In a world in which birth and hereditary wealth give political power and, presumably, personal happiness, Godwin shows us an aristocrat who is destroyed by irresponsible wealth, becomes unresponsive to domestic and social perfection, then is led once more into the chimera of unlimited wealth and its supposed power to grant unlimited happiness. Wealth isolates him from every loving social relationship: "I can no longer cheat my fancy; I know that I am alone. The creature does not exist with whom I have any common language, or any genuine sympathy." [27] St. Leon is rescued from dungeon and isolation by his own son Charles. Is this filial relationship important, or might his rescuer just as well be any other human being? The philosopher who had earlier condemned particular affections as the great barrier to universal benevolence, now penitently pleads with the astonished reader:

Let not the reader condemn me, that, endowed as I was with unlimited powers of action, I preferred a single individual, my own son, to all the world beside. Philanthropy is a godlike virtue, and can never be too loudly commended, or too ardently enjoined; but natural affection winds itself in so many folds about the heart, and is the parent of so complicated, so various and exquisite emotions, that he who should attempt to divest himself of it, will find that he is divesting himself of all that is most to be coveted in existence. . . .[28]

Moreover, this affection does not blight the growth of social sympathy; rather, indeed, do the tender duties of the family circle awaken into activity a desire to help others not akin to us.[29]

St. Leon, while enormously successful as a revelation of what a revolutionary idealist like Godwin thought about the possibilities of man's life and social usefulness, was only moderately successful as a novel, although it had its devoted readers. On one occasion Byron asked Godwin why he did not write another novel. Godwin, at that time an old man, protested that the effort would kill him. Byron replied, "And what matter? We should have another St. Leon!" [30] And the novel received the equivocal compliment of imitation in John Daly Burk's *Bethlem Gabor, Lord of Transylvania, or The Man Hating Palatine; an Historical Drama,* presented in Petersburg, Virginia, 1807.[31]

Fleetwood, *1805*

As a novelist, William Godwin was most anxious not to bore his reading audience by repeating himself. *Caleb Williams* was full of events which, while often surprising or uncommon, could have occurred within the "laws and established course of nature, as she operates in the planet we inhabit." *St. Leon,* on the other hand, was "of the miraculous class" and was designed to "mix human feelings and passions with incredible situations, and thus render them impressive and interesting." [32] Having duplicated in the novel the challenges Wordsworth and Coleridge had accepted in the Preface to the *Lyrical Ballads,* what is left? *Fleetwood: or, the New Man of Feeling,* published in two volumes in 1805,

. . . consists of such adventures, as for the most part have occurred to at least one half of the Englishmen now existing, who are of the same rank of life as my hero. Most of them have been at college, and shared in college excesses; most of them have afterward run a certain gauntlet of dissipation; most have married; and, I am afraid, there are few of the married tribe, who have not at some time or other had certain small misunderstandings with their wives;—to be sure, they have not all of them felt and acted under these trite adventures as my hero does. In this little work the reader will scarcely find anything to 'elevate and surprise'; and, if it has any merit, it must consist in the liveliness with which it brings things home to the imagination, and the reality it gives to the scenes it pourtrays.[33]

The novel shows precisely and in detail how a misanthrope of sensibility is formed. Let him be the only son of a melancholy, grieving father, and live amidst wild and magnificent scenery in Wales. Make him a solitary wanderer, a climber of mountains. Give him a tutor he can respect but not love, and surround him with peasants whom he may save from drowning but with whom he can scarcely identify himself. At the age of sixteen send him to Oxford where his strongest recollection will be of a certain Withers who wrote a heroic epic on the fifth labor of Hercules in the Augean stable. The solemn phrases, the inappropriate action described in pompous elegance, the efforts of a campus prankster, the final paroxysm of unbelieving laughter—all send the poet-author to death at the bottom of the reedy Isis.

At age twenty, Casimir Fleetwood graduated from Oxford and went to Paris to join a campus butt, Sir Charles Gleed, who, somehow was very elegant and successful in Gallic circles. There Fleetwood loves and briefly attains to a marchioness and to a countess, decides he hates women, and flees to the Alps. He meets Monsieur Ruffigny, a beloved and trusted old friend of his father's, and Ruffigny tells his story in one of the novelettes Godwin loved to embed in his narratives. For twenty years Fleetwood wanders Europe, seeking true friendship, political usefulness, and personal contentment. At forty-five he is a disillusioned misanthrope.

Volume II begins with another weary, hopeless excursion, but in it Fleetwood finds hope. Fleetwood, the misanthrope, meets Macneil, a Rousseauian lover of mankind. When Macneil's daughter is left an orphan, Fleetwood takes her father's advice and marries her. He loves her and wants to be a good husband, but the marriage is almost wrecked by his excessive sensibility. Mary chooses his old study for her own special room; she wants a kind of neighborly sociability he does not desire; his poetry reading is interrupted by her appointment to gather plants with a fifteen-year-old peasant boy. Amidst these trifling jars, an evil guest involves Mary with his own brother, exposes their supposed infidelity, and Mary is cast out by her husband. The plot is finally uncovered, and Fleetwood and Mary are reconciled. Fleetwood retains a four-hundred-pound annuity and turns an estate and income over to the young man whom he had suspected and to his bride. The evil brother dies at the hands of the public executioner; and, after an extraordinary complexity of trials, Fleetwood, the misanthrope, finally rejoins the human race.

Godwin recognized the seeming inconsistency that would reconcile a man to mankind through the power of domestic love, and in the Preface he sought to defend himself:

Certain persons, who condescend to make my supposed inconsistencies the favourite object of their research, will perhaps remark with exultation on the respect expressed in this work for marriage; and exclaim, It was not always thus! referring to the pages in which this subject is treated in the *Enquiry concerning Political Justice* for the proof of their assertion. The answer to this remark is exceedingly simple. The production referred to in it, the first foundation of its author's claim to public distinction and favour, was a treatise, aiming to ascertain what new institutions in political society might be found more conducive to general happiness than those which at present prevail. In the course of this disquisition it was enquired, whether marriage, as it stands described and supported in the laws of England, might not with advantage admit of certain modifications? Can any thing be more distinct, than such a proposition on the one hand, and a recommendation on the other that each man for himself should supersede and trample upon the institutions of the country in which he lives? A thousand things might be found excellent and salutary, if brought into general practice, which would in some cases appear ridiculous, and in others be attended with tragical consequences, if prematurely acted upon by a solitary individual. The author of *Political Justice*, as appears again and again in the pages of that work, is the last man in the world to recommend a pitiful attempt, by scattered examples to renovate the face of society, instead of endeavouring by discussion and reasoning, to effect a grand and comprehensive improvement in the sentiments of its members.[34]

The answer is perhaps not so satisfying as it is "simple." The simple fact is that in *Political Justice* Godwin had warned against the attempt at individual social changes which were not prepared for and sanctioned by a consensus of public opinion. Thus, in referring to individuals who attempt to "supersede and trample upon the institutions of the country," he is quoting his angry critics, repeating his own clear warning, and pointing to a more satisfactory biographical explanation. When Shelley ran off with Mary Godwin, he must have known that for at least fifteen years Godwin had maintained the inadvisability of individual outrages against public morality. If Shelley had followed the development of the novelist from the political thinker, he also would have been aware that marriage with Mary Wollstonecraft had taught William Godwin some rich lessons about love—lessons he revealed more clearly in his novels than in any philosophical treatise.

Once again, in *Fleetwood,* the author of *Caleb Williams* and of *St. Leon* insists that a man needs to identify himself in some meaningful way with the lives of the persons about him. Macneil diagnoses Fleetwood's distemper: "If you are now wayward and peevish and indolent and hypochondriacal, it is because you weakly hover on the outside of the pale of human society, instead of gallantly entering yourself in the ranks, and becoming one in the great congregation of man." [35] Here Godwin, in the disguise of Macneil, indicts that particularly supine form of sentimentalism, the *Weltschmerz,* which was so popular an emotional pose in his generation, and which Byron, in particular, made so popular with his own countrymen.

Fleetwood belongs to the family of those languid epicures of feeling, Goethe's Werther, Chateaubriand's René, Madame de Staël's Lord Melvil, Senancour's Obermann, and Lamartine's as yet uncreated hero, Raphael.[36] Through dissipation in Paris, the deceitfulness of mistresses, the imposture of *literateurs,* and the corruption of politics, Fleetwood tastes the bitter ashes of disillusionment. To cure boredom, he travels; but he can find nothing worthy of enjoyment. At the age of forty-five he has found no true friend or lover, no career, and no interests outside himself. At such a moment, Werther, Saint-Preux, René, Obermann, and Raphael contemplated suicide. At this point, Godwin's hero reacts violently against the Romantic agony and its frequent solution. "Suicide," he writes to a despondent friend, "is only a cowardly escape from every man's duty to do as much good as he can in the world." [37] Thus, through Macneil, Godwin meets sentimental pessimism with an equally sentimental optimism: every man is "fully prepared and eager to do a thousand virtuous acts the moment the occasion is afforded him." [38] Nevertheless, Godwin must be credited with recognizing the dangers of a current attitude and solution, and with insisting that there are more constructive responses to disillusionment than suicide.

His remarks in *Fleetwood* on youth and learning are particularly significant for the future editor of children's books. In a passage which sears like the later writings of Dickens, he describes the silk factories of Lyons. Children from four years of age and up are employed from six in the morning to six at night, with a half hour off for breakfast and an hour for dinner. For ten and one half hours each day they are set to watch fifty-six bobbins continually.[39] Concerning liberty and learning, he states categorically that

Liberty is the school of understanding. This is not enough adverted to. Every boy learns more in his hours of play than in his hours of labour. In school he lays in the materials of thinking; but in his sports he actually thinks: he whets his faculties, and he opens his eyes. The child from the moment of his birth is an experimental philosopher; he essays his organs, and his limbs, and learns the use of his muscles. Every one who will attentively observe him, will find that this is his perpetual employment. But the whole process depends upon liberty. Put him into a mill, and his understanding will improve no more than that of the horse which turns it. I know that it is said that the lower orders of the people have nothing to do with the cultivation of the understanding; though for my part I cannot see how they would be the worse for that growth of practical intellect, which should enable them to plan and provide, each one for himself, the increase of his conveniences and competence. But be it so! I know that the earth is the great Bridewell of the universe, where spirits, descended from heaven are committed to drudgery and hard labour.[40]

Besides the indignant defense of the liberty of children, an element destined to greater importance in a later phase of his publications, *Fleetwood* marks another evidence of William Godwin's decisive and significant break with the "selfish theory" of basic human motivation: "Far be it from me to assert, with certain morose and cold-blooded moralists, that our best actions are only more subtle methods by which self-love seeks its gratification." [41] Basically, the novel rejects the idea so commonly set forth in the literature of the Romantic period that any individual can afford to hold himself separate in superiority from other men. Romanticism often develops the pattern of the separated genius who, because he is so exceptional, is scorned by a dull, crass world. It often suggests that the man of creative talent should assume that he will experience some sort of martyrdom as the price for his difference from his fellows.

But Fleetwood becomes a misanthrope because he had not found a true friend. When he weds Mary he finds the one who can free the flow of his personal love, but this flow cannot stop there. "Are all the kindnesses of the human heart to be shut up within the paltry limits of consanguinity?" [42] The kindnesses of the human heart are to be released by interpersonal love, and they are to flow out through the family into the public life beyond. And, against a disillusionment that comes from passionate criticism of "Things as They Are," he insists that the ideal is to be found in the actual. A man must do the good that lies in his power, not simply despair that greater good cannot, in the present state of society, be done. It is also clear that *Fleetwood* condemns the Romantic frenzy that throws itself on the thorns of life, cherishes painful emotions, and drowns passively beneath the flood of the world's accumulated evils. Nothing must be cherished that incapacitates a man for useful, benevolent attitudes and activities!

William Hazlitt early put his sharp critical finger on Godwin's tendency to build a character entirely out of one "humour" and a plot out of one obsessive motivation: "Mr. Godwin, in all his writings, dwells upon one idea or exclusive view of a subject, aggrandizes a sentiment, exaggerates a character, or pushes an argument to extremes, and makes up by the force of style and continuity of feeling for what he wants in variety of incident or ease of manner. This necessary defect is observable in his best works, and is still more so in *Fleetwood* and *Mandeville,* the one of which, compared wtih his more admired performances, is mawkish, and the other morbid." [43]

Political Justice often seemed to push an argument not only so far as it would go logically, but also far beyond the normal affectional life of men. So the excellence of his characters is "a little overconscious," and his wronged and victimized woman "a little too ready, not only to *think,* but to *say,* how very unreasonable her husband is. . . ." The author of the *Memoir* feels that a characteristic of all Godwin's novelistic women is that "They have too keen

a sense of the *Rights of Women!*" [44] This serious intentness upon a
single-minded didactic purpose tends to produce volumes quite
without humor. Perhaps the most remarkable thing, therefore,
about *Fleetwood* is the Oxford episode of the Greek drama based
on the Herculean cleansing of the stables of Augeas. Indeed it
ends tragically and contributes solidly to the hero's disillusionment
with mankind, yet it is brilliantly satirical and full of a rich, almost
Rabelaisian humor that shows Godwin's affinity to Swift. Godwin
even enriched the passage to the point of preparing a hilarious
specimen ode supposedly taken from the ponderously sober student tragedy.

Godwin's unfortunate habit of embedding undeveloped novelettes in his longer narratives appears in the third volume, and it is
an oddity of the first volume that it recounts the history of two of
Fleetwood's intimate love affairs, with full recognition of what
they contribute to his budding misanthropy, but without employing a single word of dialogue. The Preface is more characteristic,
with its impassioned and apocalyptic vision of the England Godwin knew compared to the earlier England he had read about and
revered:

I saw that the public character of England, as it exists in the best pages
of our history, was gone. I perceived that we were grown a commercial
and arithmetical nation; and that, as we extended the superficies of our
empire, we lost its moral sinews and its strength. The added numbers
which have been engrafted upon both houses of parliament, have destroyed the health and independence of its legislature; the wealth of
either India has been poured upon us, to smother that free spirit which
can never be preserved but in a moderate fortune; contractors, direc-
tors and upstarts, men fattened on the vitals of their fellow-citizens,
have taken the place which was once filled by the Wentworths, the
Seldens, and the Hydes. By the mere project, the most detestable and
fatal that was ever devised, of England borrowing of the individuals
who constitute England, and accumulating what is called a national
debt, she has mortgaged her sons to an interminable slavery.[45]

Mandeville, *1817*

In his Preface to *Mandeville: A Tale of the Seventeenth Century in England* (1817), William Godwin attributed the plot of

the novel to ideas arising from reading Charles Brockden Brown's *Wieland* and James Kennedy Bailie's *De Montfort*. It was particularly gracious of him to acknowledge his debt to Brown, since on no occasion does he indicate the American novelist's indebtedness to him. In a letter to William Dunlap, Brown disclosed his plan to write a novel in Godwinian style.[46] Although nothing came of the original plan, his novel *Wieland* is almost always described as a Godwinian novel, clearly indebted to *Political Justice* for philosophic ideas and to *Caleb Williams* for plot and style.

In 1816 Godwin had visited Scotland, met Walter Scott, and arranged with Mr. Constable, the bookseller, for the publication of *Mandeville* the next year. The dominant tone of the three-volume work is indicated by the motto from the Biblical book of Exodus: "And the waters of that fountain were bitter: and they said, Let the name of it be called Marah." *Mandeville,* like *St. Leon* and *Fleetwood,* is the study of a man in tragic isolation from his fellows. Like *Caleb Williams,* the dominant motive of the leading character is a false sense of personal and family honor. As in all Godwin novels, there is the psychological and sociological analysis of the environmental elements that form a particular kind of character. The Godwinian artistic canon of a single concentrated effect is everywhere noticeable.

When Mandeville was only three years of age, he was the horrified witness to the massacre of his parents. For the next eight or nine years he was exposed to the influences of a melancholy uncle with whom he lived in the close seclusion of a gloomy, depressing mansion. Out of his boyhood enthusiasm for the chivalric world, he gave his heart and life-allegiance to the cause of Charles Stuart; but, by the public misunderstanding that is a composite villain in Godwin's works, Mandeville is suspected of being, and is slandered as, an anti-royalist spy. In the end, he sees his sister, Henrietta, the only person he has really loved in all the world, married to a man whom he considers the prime mover in all his misfortunes. But this sorrow, real though it may be, is based on the same kind of supposititious evidence he had condemned in the vulgar crowd. As he had been misunderstood and slandered, so he misunderstands and slanders, wounding most the person he most loves.

[103]

Mandeville's sister Henrietta seems most often to be the bearer of the Godwinian philosophic line in the novel. By virtue of his parents' massacre, the recluse uncle, the gloomy mansion, and the misunderstanding of society, Mandeville becomes a misanthrope —not of course, because of any personal tendency, but always because of the forces that play upon him. Henrietta is the bearer of the truth that is everywhere its own strongest witness and, when adequately presented, must be received by men of good will. "By the very constitution of our being we are compelled to delight in society," she argues. "If man could meet man on an uninhabited island how would he rejoice in his good fortune!" If this is true on the unusual level, it is equally true on the usual: "Oh, then, how should beings of this wonderful structure, hail each other's presence, love each other's good, and strain their utmost nerve, to defend each other from injury." Henrietta is a confirmed Godwinian as she argues for the moral blamelessness of the individual and the moral responsibility of society. Man, she proclaims, "is just what his nature and circumstances have made him. . . . If he is corrupt, it is because he has been corrupted. . . . Give him a different education, place him under other circumstances . . . and he would be altogether a different creature." If, because of chance, circumstance, and error of judgment, he has transgressed the rules of society or the sovereignty of truth, "He is to be pitied therefore, not regarded with hatred; to be considered with indulgence, not made an object of revenge; to be reclaimed with mildness, to be gradually inspired with confidence; to be enlightened and better informed as to the mistakes into which he has fallen, not made the butt and object of our ferocity." [47]

Shelley was so stirred by Henrietta's Godwinian eloquence that he wrote: "The pleadings of Henrietta to Mandeville, after his recovering from madness, in favour of virtue and benevolent energy, compose, in every respect, the most perfect and beautiful piece of writing of modern times." His review makes it clear that he recognized the voice of the political scientist behind the accents of the sister: "It is the genuine doctrine of *Political Justice*, presented in one perspicacious and impressive river, and clothed in such enchanting melody of language as seems, not less than the writings of Plato, to realize those lines of Milton:

> How charming is divine Philosophy!
> Not harsh and crabbed—
> But musical as is Apollo's lute." [48]

This comment was taken from a long review of *Mandeville*, sent by Shelley to *The Examiner* on December 28, 1817. A short review, published in *The Morning Chronicle*, December 9, 1817, arose out of the usual comedy of error, misunderstanding, and incompatibility that continually erupted around Godwin and his son-in-law. On December 1, Shelley wrote to William Godwin: "Mandeville has arrived this evening. Mary is now reading it— and I am like a man on the brink of a precipice. . . ." Six days later, having finished reading the book, Shelley wrote Godwin, praising the novel highly. Godwin evidently extracted the laudatory comments from the letter, changed the references to the author from second to third person, and sent the unauthorized review to *The Morning Chronicle*, which printed it on December 9, with the heading "Extract of a Letter from Oxfordshire." Shelley, who must have seen the excerpts from his personal letter in the newspaper, wrote an exasperated but generous note to Godwin on the eleventh: "If I had believed it possible you should send any part of my letter to the *Chronicle*, I should have expressed more fully my sentiments of *Mandeville*, and of the author. . . . The effect of your favourable consideration . . . has emboldened me to write—not a volume but a more copious statement of my feelings as they were excited by *Mandeville*. This I have sent to the *Examiner*." [49]

Once again it is important to note that, when the philosopher moves from political ethics to art, he tends also to move from an almost legal intellectual consistency to a Romantic and even sentimental excess of feeling. If we are not to condemn the criminal for his crime, we may run to the other extreme and weep tears of compassion for him. Falkland, St. Leon, Fleetwood, and Mandeville are all "men of acute sensibility" in their response to suffering and adulation of nobility, in their total lack of reserve as they break down in pity or break out in raptures. St. Leon is extravagant in his grief for his mother; Travers, in *Deloraine*, and Julian, in *Cloudesley*, are equally uninhibited upon the death of a friend. Haunters of graveyards, St. Leon times his visit for the hour "when nature assumed her darkest times," and Travers views William's grave "by the light of the starry heavens." [50]

Lord Alton is the man-of-taste-and-feeling when he describes a fair young Greek whom he has rescued from her Turkish pursuers: "Beauty in sorrow is the adversary that has thrown down its arms, and no longer defies us to conquer its powers. It is the weak and tender flower, illustrious in its lowliness, that asks for a friendly hand to raise its drooping head." [51] When Mandeville finds his beloved Mary in a peasant cottage nursing a sick friend, he gushes: "It was a sight on which an angel might have dwelt with rapture." [52] It is curious that at no point of the narrative does Godwin recall his beloved wife's reaction to high-flown gallantry directed at women. Mary Wollstonecraft wrote with lethal indignation about the language addressed to women by a certain popular preacher, Dr. Fordyce:

Florid appeals are made to heaven, and to the *beauteous innocents,* the fairest images of heaven here below, whilst sober sense is left far behind. . . . I particularly object to the lover-like phrases of pumped-up passion, which are everywhere interspersed. . . . Speak to them [women] the language of truth and soberness, and away with the lullaby strains of condescending endearment! Let themselves be taught to respect themselves as rational creatures, and not led to have a passion for their own insipid persons. It moves my gall to hear a preacher descanting on dress and needlework: and still more to hear him address the *British fair,* and the *fairest of the fair,* as if they had only feelings.[53]

Perhaps had Mary survived, her critical sense would have helped Godwin find some midway point between the cold and forbidding legalism of which he is usually accused, and the extravagant and rhetorical sensibility which has usually gone un-noted in his novels.

Cloudesley, 1830

Cloudesley: a Tale, "By the Author of *Caleb Williams,*" appeared in London in 1830. A minor part of the tale came from the *Memoirs of an Unfortunate Young Noble Returned from Thirteen Years Slavery in America* (1743), but the main narrative is pure Godwin. Lord Alton, heir to the earldom of Danvers, marries a lovely young Greek, Irene Colocotroni. With the customary exaggerated pride of a Godwin hero, he strikes his rival, Fabroni, and is killed in the subsequent duel, victim of the man who killed him —but a victim also of a tradition of personal and family honor, and of society.

Volume II opens with the death of the widow, in childbirth; whereupon her brother-in-law sends Lord Alton's child, Julian, off to the Continent with a confidential secretary, Cloudesley, and assumes the title. Cloudesley had been shaped into the misanthropic tool for such a function by an unjust prison sentence. Volume II ends as Cloudesley, reclaimed from misanthropy by domestic affection, determines to return to England to win Julian his rightful place. Volume III tells the morbid tale of the deaths of each of the unrightful Lord Danvers' children and heirs, by mysterious maladies, which the father of course relates to his crime against the true heir. In the meantime, Julian has joined the camp of Count Federigo, who is actually the notorious bandit leader St. Elmo. Cloudesley, upon his return from Ireland, locates Julian just before his own death. St. Elmo is to be executed, along with eight banditti and Julian, supposedly one of the robber band. Meadows, emissary from the expiring Lord Danvers, reveals the secret identity to the British consul, and Julian is freed. The persecuted youth is now the fortunate heir to the earldom.

The novel is full of characteristic Godwin patterns. There is the youth trained in the tradition of false honor and chivalry, who falls a victim, not to his own folly, but to his mistaken education. There is the persecuted youth who comes into his own through the power of truth. Cloudesley is a misanthrope, not specifically because he is the victim of an unjust prison sentence, but because, generally any condemnation of man by man is unjust, and any attempt at punishment or forced reformation of the criminal is bound to fail. Having lost his innocent faith in the goodness of the world, and having been initiated into its capricious evil, he is reclaimed for the human race by the power of love. His surrogate fatherhood of Julian heals the wounds of human injustice and frees the floods of love, not only to his cheated ward, but in universal benevolence. Julian's guardian, Borromeo, converted from harsh misanthropy by the restitution of the estate to its rightful owner, confesses that "the world is not what I took it to be." By which he does not mean, as Cloudesley might once have said, that it is worse than he thought, but infinitely better. "I have acted alternately the part of the master and the slave. . . . The true key to the universe is love. That levels all inequalities . . . and brings human beings of every age and station into a state of brotherhood . . . the man that is austere to his fellow mortal is . . . the practical atheist." [54]

In his delineation of St. Elmo, Godwin goes beyond his usual theme of the outlaw who is the product of a faulty education and an unjust society. Casting aside all restraint, he depicts a noble outlaw who "would have been distinguished among savages, among the feudal followers of Charlemagne, or among the crusaders, as well as in the wars of Camillus and Scipio, or in the heroic games of Olympia." [55] The complete individualist, St. Elmo regarded so-called civilized society as a mass conspiracy against the freedom of the individual, and had early made up his mind to pay no attention to its laws. Thus St. Elmo is in the family line, not only of Rousseau's noble savage and of Godwin's *Political Justice*, but also of the Romantic fervor for the sovereignty of the individual.

An anonymous review of *Cloudesley* in the *Edinburgh Review* considered this novel as better written than *Caleb Williams:* "The expression is everywhere terse, vigorous, elegant:—a polished mirror without a wrinkle." [56] But the characterization (perhaps particularly that of the noble St. Elmo), led the reviewer to quip: "All his characters are patterns of vice or virtue. They are carried to extremes,—they are abstractions of woe, miracles of wit and gaiety. . . . This is not like a veteran in the art, but like the raptures of some boarding-school girl in love with every new face or dress she sees. . . ." [57] Moreover, the form of the novel is notoriously, even magnificently bad. There is no one hero, and the attention of the reader wavers among Lord Alton, Meadows, Cloudesley, St. Elmo, and Julian.

Meadows begins [the narrative] with an account of himself, and a topographical description of the Russian empire, which has nothing to do with the subject; and nearly through the remainder of the work, listens to a speech of Lord Danvers, recounting his own history and that of Julian, which lasts for six hundred pages without interruption or stop. It is the longest parenthesis in a narrative that ever was known. Meadows then emerges from his *incognito* once more, as if he had been hid behind a curtain, and gives the coup-de-grace to his own auto-biography, and the lingering suffering of his patron.[58]

The same reviewer describes Godwin's main characteristic as a thinker and writer by using "the pugilistic phrase, an *out-and-outer*." *Political Justice* proved to the reviewer that "Mr. Godwin was the first *whole-length* broacher of the doctrines of *Utility*. He took the whole duty of man—all other passions, affections, rules, weaknesses, oaths, gratitude, promises, friendship, natural piety, patriotism—infused them in the glowing caldron of universal benevolence, and ground them into powder under the unsparing weight of the conviction of the individual understanding." [59] Since he never stops until he "reaches the verge of all we hate," it is scarcely odd that he occasionally loses his balance and topples over. "Some leading truth, some master-passion, is the secret of his daring and his success. . . ." [60] Thus the reviewer classifies *Cloudesley* as a "dissertation on remorse." With quite modern critical acumen he notes that "from the philosophical to the romantic visionary, there was perhaps but one step." [61]

It is, perhaps, because Godwin took that step that he had so profound an effect upon his contemporaries. They thought they were approaching the nature and destiny of man from the most rigidly logical point of view. In actual fact they were moving along a pathway of the most visionary idealism, of faith in truth and reason, and of a too-sentimental compassion for life's sufferers.

Deloraine, *1833*

The selection from the writings of Pope chosen by William Godwin as the motto of *Deloraine* (1833) is ominous in a familiar way: "Why that bosom gored?/ Why dimly gleams the visionary sword?" The reader who has faithfully perused *Caleb Williams, St. Leon, Fleetwood, Mandeville,* and *Cloudesley* is thoroughly prepared for the suggestion of a passionate crime of violence, committed by a man who is no more guilty than the sword with which he did the deed. In the Preface, Godwin tells us that the rude outline of the tale was first committed to paper on January 17, 1830. Although he had just completed *Cloudesley,* he felt that the "Great Unknown" (obviously Sir Walter Scott) "had sufficiently shewn that it was not absolutely necessary for the mind of an author to lie fallow for years, between the conclusion of one work of fiction and the commencement of another. And, old as I was, and little as it might become me in other respects to put forward a comparison between myself and the writer now recently deceased [Scott died September 21, 1832], I felt an ambition to shew that I upon occasion could be no less unintermitted in the invention of a narrative." Godwin then refers to circumstances which compelled him to lay aside the task for a time—circumstances which he ought not to intrude upon the minds of his readers, but which must refer to the death of his son William in the fall of 1832. Now that many months had passed, the author hopes he has resumed his task "with no mixture of irresoluteness, and . . . with no flagging wing. . . ." [62]

The wing does not flag, but neither does it lay out any new path of flight. Deloraine, after an indulged but lonely childhood, enters the House of Commons and marries Emilia Fitzcharles. They enjoy wonderful happiness in an idyllic marriage of utter frankness, sharing, and trust. Their daughter, Catherine, is left with a family friend, Mrs. Catherine Fanshaw, while the parents vacation on the Continent. Emilia, wet through by a sudden storm on a lake, has a miscarriage and dies. Deloraine, sinking beneath this sudden misfortune, lies sick with typhus fever, with a young friend as his only companion. When Deloraine is forty-two, he meets Margaret Borradale, twenty-three. With his usual bad habit of the embedded novelette, Godwin tells Margaret's sad tale. She was saved from falling off a cliff by a young friend, William, with whom she promptly fell in love. But she was affianced to be the bride of Lord Borradale's son. She did not refuse, but sank into such bad health that it finally became apparent to all that she would die. The engagement to Lord Borradale's son was broken, and William was called to her side. He came, but his ship sank within sight of Plymouth harbor, where Margaret awaited her lover.

In Volume II a pale and shadowy Margaret is wed to Deloraine. But shortly we learn that William was picked up by an English frigate. He reappears, surprises Margaret in her garden; she faints; Deloraine arrives, draws the wrong conclusions, and shoots the supposed molester of his wife. Volume III becomes a novel of pursuit, as Deloraine and his daughter flee from the avenging Creole, Travers, and Margaret's faithful servant, Ambrose. After finding that no shelter shields them from pursuit, they are taken aboard a boat belonging to Thornton, the same young friend who had nursed Deloraine through an illness. Deloraine finally decides on the ingenious plan of becoming a master of disguise and of living in the immediate fellowship of his pursuers. Catherine has a better idea. With high courage and the ardor of a Godwinian philosopher, she goes to Travers and challenges him to end the search. Travers melts at the sovereign truth, astonished at the picture of himself as a sub-human bloodhound. Catherine marries Thornton, and the three—father, daughter, son-in-law— live on Thornton's estate in Holland, where Catherine bears a son and Deloraine makes the expiation of unending remorse.

In this comparatively well-knit tale many characteristic Godwinian touches reappear. Deloraine's dream-world of idyllic marriage and security is destroyed by a wind on a lake. Margaret's simple dream of love and marriage goes down with a sinking ship. The plot hinges on the wrong reading of external phenomena— the assumption that William necessarily perished on the *Roebuck,* and the murder of a former lover who is supposedly molesting the woman he is supporting after her fainting fit. There is the passionate crime of violence, with its overtones of marriage as the possession of property and the defense of an old-fashioned concept of personal honor. Travers, the bloodhound, became a misanthrope from watching the sad fate of his father, a philanthropist who was rejected by those he had tried to help and who died of a broken heart. Travers is converted from a misanthropic career of pursuit and restored to the human race by the power of the word of truth spoken in perfect sincerity by a lovely maiden. There is also the usual Godwinian confusion of heroes and villains. Everyone— William, Margaret, Deloraine, Travers—did what he had been conditioned to do, and was not really guilty. Moreover, once he was given an adequate presentation of the higher truth, he embraced it eagerly and instantaneously. "Why [was] that bosom gored?" Because life had prepared men just as men had prepared steel to form the "visionary sword." Sword and men were both instruments—not agents. Murdered and murderer were both victims; neither one is guilty or innocent.

Imitations and Anti-Godwinian Novels

In 1801, in his reply to Dr. Parr's *Spital Sermon,* Godwin declared: "The cry spread like a general infection, and I have been told that not even a petty novel . . . now ventures to aspire to favour, unless it contains some expression of dislike and abhorrence to the new philosophy, and its chief (or shall I say its most voluminous?) English adherent." The many imitations of Godwin's style and philosophy express the flattery of imitation; the anti-Godwinian novels express the reaction against the political and social liberal. In September, 1795, Charles Brockden Brown wrote to William Dunlap, painter and dramatist:

Soon after my return [from New York], I began the design of which we talked so much. I had planned so that I could finish a work equal in content to *Caleb Williams* in less than six weeks; and I wrote a quantity equivalent to ten of his pages daily, till the hot weather and inconvenient circumstances obliged me to relax my diligence. Great expedition does not seem very desirable. Tenets so momentous require a leisurely and deep examination; and much meditation, reading and writing, I presume, are necessary to render my system of morality perfect in all its parts, and to acquire a full and luminous conviction; but I have stopped—I go on, though less precipitately than at first, and I hope finally to produce something valuable for its utility.[63]

Although nothing came of this early project, Godwin's style of writing and his political theories undoubtedly were strong influences not only on Brown's *Wieland,* but on *Ormond* and *Arthur Mervyn.* As Godwin dominates his reader, holds him by a hypnotic interest, even terrorizes him in the Gothic manner, so Brown treats his readers. The same headlong, intense style hurries the reader along the strand of plot. There are no heroes and no villains; all characters are victims of their environments. And, therefore, one ought to judge and punish the erroneous social institutions that formed them rather than punish the predetermined characters.

The dependence of Mary Hays's *Memoirs of Emma Courtney* on *The Rights of Woman* and *Political Justice* has been mentioned in Chapter III. George Walker's *The Vagabond* makes a personal attack on Godwin in 1799, after Walker had slavishly

[112]

copied the plot of *Caleb Williams* in his own novel *Theodore Cyphon* (1796). In 1800 Elizabeth Hamilton published *Memoirs of Modern Philosophers,* replete with thinly veiled pen-portraits of Godwin and other contemporary social and political thinkers. In her later *Letters of a Hindoo Rajah,* she made unmistakable fun of Godwin's version of the Helvetian doctrine that a man is the sum total of all the influences that play upon him from the moment of his birth: "Miss Ardent:—'According to the arguments of the young philosopher, I see no reason why, by a proper course of education, a monkey may not be a Minister of State, or a good Lord Chancellor of England.' " [64] Godwin seems never to have stooped to making the obvious reply.

Edward Dubois, in *St. Godwin, by Count Reginald de St. Leon* (1800) puts this boast on Godwin's lips: "with a terrible pother about what nobody could understand; namely: the *absoluteness of necessity,* the *perfectibility of man,* and the *omnipotence of truth,* I opposed all political and moral order, and endeavoured to overturn every system that time and experience had sanctioned and approved." [65] In a double reference to Charles Lamb's description of the *Political Justice* passage concerning the Abbé Fénelon, Dubois shows the lover Frederick trying to decide whether to rescue his fiancée or his father—while the house burns down. Mrs. Opie, in her novel *Adeline Mowbray* (1804) represents Godwin as a well-intentioned man who had been imposed upon by a cold-blooded, calculating villian with a specious doctrine of philanthropy. The theory was chosen because of its congeniality to his unprincipled nature, and the villain deliberately employs the doctrines of *Political Justice* in order to destroy the moral scruples of his intended victims. [66]

Benjamin Silliman, in *Letters of Shahcoolen, a Hindu Philosopher Residing in Philadelphia; to His Friend El Hassan, an Inhabitant of Delhi,* notes that the "new Philosophy has spread, in a greater or less degree, over the whole of civilized Europe, and it is *inculcated,* and believed by multitudes in America . . ." [67] it is the ruling topic of discussion; it is perpetually contested and advocated, by the learned and the great; while the lowest classes of society . . . implicitly believe the dogmas, which they are taught." [68] Because of the spread of Godwinian philosophy, the "Bible is the subject of ridicule and blasphemous levity," priests are "loaded with obloquy and contempt," churches are used for "profane occasions," the national leaders are "the jest of every vulgar tongue." [69] "I am told that the state of things which I have described, is imputed in part, to the influence of the new philosophy. It is the spirit of this philosophy to reduce all things to one common level; to pull down the Gods from their thrones, and to trample the kings of the earth in the dust. It interferes in every concern of public, and of private life; and aims at a total change in every department of society." [70]

Other novels of imitation and abuse include Charles Lucas' *The Infernal Quixote,* Charles Lloyd's *Edmund Oliver,* Mrs. West's *A Tale of the Times,* the anonymous *Doreathea, or A Ray of the New Light,* and the also anonymous *The Citizen's Daughter.* Such are the "novels of buffoonery and scandal" to which Godwin refused to reply in his answer to Dr. Parr's *Spital Sermon.*[71]

II *The Stage*

William Godwin entered Hoxton College as a student in September, 1773. The following summer, he planned to compose "two tragedies, one on the subject of Iphigenia in Aulis, and the other on the death of Caesar. . . ." [72] For most students of literature, Godwin is known primarily as the major philosophic influence on Wordsworth and Shelley, as the author of *Political Justice,* and as the writer of two fairly successful novels and of many that are now generally forgotten. But he is also associated with the stage, first, through his own unsuccessful plays, *Antonio* (1800) and *Faulkener* (1807), and derivatively through George Colman's dramatization of *Caleb Williams* under the title *The Iron Chest,* and Wordsworth's poetic drama *The Borderers* (1796), a statement of the poet's re-evaluation of Godwinian philosophy.

Antonio, *1800*

Godwin considered *Antonio: A Tragedy in Five Acts* his best work, but his contemporaries considered it a failure—and posterity has seen no reason to revise their estimate. In the play, Helena D'Almanza was promised on her father's deathbed to her brother Antonio's best friend, Roderigo. But, while Roderigo and Antonio are developing great reputations as warriors, Helena falls in love with Don Gusman. It is in every way an appropriate union, and the king releases his ward from her deathbed filial vow and approves the marriage to the noble Gusman. Antonio returns from the wars, leaving Roderigo on the field. The latter has had great difficulties and sorrows, but Antonio has comforted him with the thought of his eventual marriage to Helena. When Antonio finds his sister married, he furiously considers her marriage invalid and a betrayal of her promise to her father. He kidnaps his sister from her husband's home and demands that the king annul the marriage. He no longer feels her worthy of his friend, but requires that she must suffer, and then perhaps enter a convent for a life of expiation. The king is patient at first with the returned military hero, but he finally reaffirms his first judgment that the precontract with Roderigo was not binding and that the marriage to Gusman is valid. Whereupon, Antonio breaks through the cordon of guards, kills his sister, and gives himself up to the punishment due.

Godwin's diary records constant and laborious work on the play, with continual revisions and polishing. When it was performed on December 13, 1800, John Kemble and Mrs. Siddons took the leading roles of Antonio and Helena. The tragedy was in blank verse, with the prologue and epilogue written by Charles Lamb. There was no second performance of the play, and another poetic drama by Godwin, *Abbas, King of Persia,* was rejected for performance the following year. The public catastrophe of the closing of Godwin's play was recorded by Charles Lamb many years afterward in the *London Magazine* for April 10, 1822, in an essay entitled "The Old Actors," which is sometimes reprinted in the collected *Essays of Elia.*

We are also indebted to the gently acid pen of Lamb for the raptures and disillusionment of Anne Seward, the Minerva of Lichfield. When she received a copy of *Antonio,* with leaves uncut, she exulted, "The characteristic strength, the depth of thought, the heart-grappling interest, and the terrible graces of *Caleb Williams* and *St. Leon* will nobly support the tragic muse. Yes: they will revive her laurels, withered, and in the dust since Jephson forsook her. . . ." After she read the play, she mourned, "O, my stars, what short-lived exultation! How are the mighty fallen and the weapons of genius blunted!" [73]

Another female admirer, Mrs. Inchbald, received a similar volume and, after reading it, wrote a superbly ironic note of thanks:

LEINSTER SQUARE
5th of January, 1801

DEAR SIR,

I thank you for the play of Antonio, as I feel myself flattered by your remembrance of me; and I most sincerely wish you joy of having produced a work which will protect you from being classed with the successful dramatists of the present day, but which will hand you down to posterity among the honored few who, during the past century, have totally failed in writing for the stage.

Your very humble Servant, E. INCHBALD.[74]

Although a failure on the stage, the tragedy was quite as successful as the novels in presenting the characteristic ideas of the political philosopher and moralist. Antonio, another Falkland, is misled by a mistaken idea of chivalric conduct and a too-strict interpretation of personal and family honor. He considers the marital pre-contract sanctified by the express wish of his dying father. The law of fifteenth-century Spain considers the absolute power of the king quite adequate to set aside the pre-contract and to bless another marriage. But Godwin, of course, would point out that this is a classic case of being bound by promises and contracts which restrict both growth and freedom. This was his criticism of marriage in *Political Justice*, and it is documented in *Antonio*. Antonio is also one of those strange Godwinian characters with an obsession: Caleb with his curiosity, Falkland with his honor, and now Antonio with his thorough-going morality—his insistence that his sister is an adulteress and the king an accessory in the breaking of the most sacred of vows. When he is unsuccessful in separating the parties legally or by persuasion, the only thing left to do is to separate them by the death of his sister. Here, again, is the double theme of the logic which is carried to disastrous social extremes and of the villain who is to be pitied because he is the victim of a wrong theory of education.

Faulkener, *1804*

The Godwin diaries for 1804 indicate that, after the publication of *Chaucer*, the novel *Fleetwood* occupied most of the author's

time and attention. But the play *Faulkener,* a tragedy, was also
completed in the same year, although not performed at the Theatre Royal, Drury Lane, until December 16, 1807. Thomas Holcroft, close friend of Godwin, was an accomplished and successful
playwright, so the unpublished and unperformed drama was sent
to him for final polishing for the stage. But Holcroft, deliberately
or unintentionally misunderstanding the intention of the author,
remodeled the entire play, and rewrote a considerable portion of
it, depending, of course, on Godwin's basic materials. Had the
resultant product of this friendly collaboration been successful,
Godwin would probably have expressed great gratitude to his
friend, for he was always quite willing to admit sources and assist-
ants. But *Faulkener* failed, and instead of praise, great wrath fell
upon the head of the devoted friend; and the assumption was that
the polishing and remodeling were responsible for the failure.
Holcroft, who had known Godwin for a long time and owed him
many personal debts of gratitude, bore all blame with dignity and
forbearance.

When *Faulkener* was played at Drury Lane, it was received
with some popular favor, and repeated for several nights; but it
never became a part of the permanent repertoire. Again Charles
Lamb wrote the Prologue in rhymed couplets. The Epilogue was
spoken by Mrs. Henry Siddons, who played the Countess Orsini.
Another Epilogue had been written by the celebrated physician
John Walcot, M.D., but it arrived too late for the opening night.
With characteristic frankness, Godwin explained in the Preface
that "The following Tragedy is founded upon an incident in a
novel commonly said to be written by Daniel Defoe, *Roxana, or
the Fortunate Mistress.*" He proceeds to explain the odd critical
phrase "commonly said to be written by Daniel Defoe." Of this
novel there are three editions. The first, 1724, breaks off abruptly.
The second, 1745, is the only complete one. Mr. Noble, a bookseller in Holborn, "a well-known publisher of new trash, and of old
novels new vamped, about forty years ago, printed a third edition
in 1775. One curious circumstance is that Defoe died in 1731,
fourteen years before the publication of the complete edition. Is
he therefore the true author of the additional part? . . . The style
certainly bears a most striking resemblance to that of the unques-
tioned productions of Defoe. . . ." The Preface also indicates that

Godwin began his play in verse, but that he soon became discouraged and wrote the remainder in prose. Then he rewrote the whole in prose, inserting only a "few passages which had been originally written in verse, and with which I was not wholly displeased."

The tragedy is powerful, but the subject is disagreeable. Arabella, countess Orsini, was formerly Mrs. Faulkener, a widow. In her lonely, unprotected state, she accepted an illicit romance with the exiled Charles Stuart and, as a result, was deprived by the law of the custody of her infant son by her previous husband. When she later marries the Count Orsini, a rigidly conventional gentleman, she withholds information about her secret past. Although happily and securely married, she is the prey of remorse for her past misdeeds and is tormented by curiosity about, and longing for, the son of whom she had deprived herself. Into this secret guilt the son appears in the person of Captain Faulkener, just returned from the war. Like all Godwinian heroes, he is obsessed with the need to uncover the secret truth. He slays Count Orsini in the inevitable Godwinian moment of criminal passion.

Perhaps the most notable thing about the drama is the underscoring of a Godwin complex. A Godwin hero is incapable of "leaving well enough alone." He must discover the truth, which then lays upon him an unsavory requirement for violence, revenge, and the sacrifice of life on the altar of a false honor. Faulkener, successful, young, handsome, in love, has all the world before him. But everything told in secret—for Godwin's characters—clamors obsessively to be shouted from the housetops, and all is then lost in a vain attempt to right the wrongs of the past, and present good is sacrificed to dead disasters. There is a marked resemblance here to the plays of Sophocles as well as to the prose works of Robert Penn Warren because of the constant theme of present order disturbed by the eruption of a past which will not stay dead, and of life sacrificed to poorly understood concepts of justice and honor.

The Iron Chest: a Play, in Three Acts, 1796

Although not a play written by William Godwin, *The Iron Chest* cannot be ignored in any consideration of Godwin's productions for the stage. George Colman, the playwright, states in his opening remarks: "The groundwork of this play is taken from Mr. Godwin's celebrated novel of *Caleb Williams*. Few works have been read with more intensity and delight than this extraordinary tale. It is the perfection of absorbing interest, ingenious arrangement, masterly delineation of character, and forcible language. It is art; but art, be it remembered, is the handmaid of nature." Mr. Colman exhibited sound judgment in dramatizing such an essentially dramatic tale, but the technique he used so well on previous plays deserted him and his play was a failure—however a failure often revived in England and America. Having borrowed the plot from another, he attempted to blame the failure on still another, in an angry tirade against the leading actor, Mr. Kemble, whose acting he supposed to be the reason for the play's mortifying failure.[75]

The drama omits the motifs of flight and pursuit entirely. It reaches a climax with the visit of Falkland's brother, the false accusation of Caleb, and the final breakdown of Falkland when his dagger is found among the things he had hastily secreted in Caleb's box—*The Iron Chest*. In the novel, Falkland's remorse stemmed, not so much from the murder of Squire Barnabas Tyrrel, which he considered due to his wounded honor, but rather from the execution of the innocent Hawkins and his son. They were victims that his determination upon revenge could not have taken into account. But Sir Edward Mortimer, in Colman's dramatization, is remorseful for his assassination of Tyrrel, and so the dynamic of the structure is weakened and the philosophic groundwork is diluted.

Two personal items are related to *The Iron Chest*. It was originally presented at the Theatre Royal, Drury Lane, Saturday, March 12, 1796; when it was presented in New York, in 1807, Thomas Cooper, one of the distinguished tragedians of the early American theater, played the role of Mortimer. This is the same Thomas Cooper who lived with Godwin after his father's death in the East Indies. Thus one of Godwin's "young men" had the privilege of playing a theatrical role based upon a characterization by his own benefactor and surrogate father.

The other item is less pleasant and delineates the little flea bites of fame that afflict even a philosopher. When *The Iron Chest* was presented for the first time, William Godwin expressed himself

most acrimoniously concerning the author. The reason for his bit-
terness was that the author of the drama had sent the author of
the novel neither tickets for a box nor an order for admission to
the production.

The Borderers, *1796*

When Wordsworth left Annette Vallon and Captain Michel
Beaupuy in France, it was December of 1792. The young man
was bewildered by his sense of guilt, conflicting loyalties, and the
competitiveness between personal and social duties. The radical
new philosophy of William Godwin captured the returned Eng-
lishman and, with its doctrine of the obligation to break promises
that inhibit growth, set him free from Annette. With its emphasis
on the particular affections as the chief enemies of universal benevolence, it also released him to the stirring world currents of his
day. The Godwinian philosophy was operative in his next important poem, "Guilt and Sorrow," with its portrayal of the bitter
sufferings of the poor victims of war and the vicious injustices of
the penal code. But the poem tended to a confused morality by its
assumption that good and evil are simply the absence or presence
of pain, establishing a similarity of source that blunts the distinction between right and wrong action. There seems to have followed a period in which Wordsworth wrestled with the problem
of the relationship of a sovereign and absolute reason to the heart
and the soul, a problem which found no solution in Godwin's philosophy but is so clearly important in man's life.

The Borderers, a five-act play which followed the poem "Guilt
and Sorrow," both exhibits and rejects Godwinian influences.
Godwinism had seemed to set Wordsworth free from his remorse
over his abandonment of Annette Vallon. But the mental adjust-
ment was not powerful enough to keep remorse from returning.
So in this essentially inward, personal drama, quite undramatic in
a theatrical sense, Wordsworth courageously faced his dilemma
and Godwin's teachings and came away with the conviction that
reason must be linked with "universal heart!" He retained his faith
in Godwin's social humanitarianism; but he had grave doubts of
the power of reason, unaided by emotion, and of the perfectibility
of man, without a long period of gradual growth.

CHAPTER 5

History for Children and Adults

". . . the great *mormo* set up to terrify all England, some forty years ago . . . most people felt of Mr. G. with the same alienation and horror as of a ghoul, or a bloodless vampyre, or the monster created by Frankenstein."

THOMAS DE QUINCEY, *Collected Writings*, (1889-1890)

I *History for Children*

WHEN the time came for the widow of Percy Bysshe Shelley to choose a school for their surviving son, someone suggested that he should go to a school where he would be free to think for himself. "To think for himself!" exclaimed the woman who was the daughter of the unique Mary Wollstonecraft and the unique William Godwin, the widow of the unique Percy Shelley, and the author of the unique *Frankenstein*. "Oh my God, teach him to think like other people!" Mary Shelley knew the joys and the perils of independence, and she wanted something different for her boy. Everyone she knew intimately had been an independent thinker, heroic, never ceasing "from mental fight." But for her son she desired the settled calm of an ordinary boyhood and a commonplace life.[1]

Her father, on the other hand, never faltered in his faith. When all the radical enthusiasm for a new society had been quenched by the excesses of the French Revolution and terrorized by Franco-phobia; when Wordsworth and Southey and Coleridge had all jettisoned their youthful dreams and become pillars of the established order, Godwin still stood firmly by an unreconstructed belief in the perfectibility of man and in the fluidity of the social order. Some explanation of this persistent hopefulness may be found in his childhood.

In writing about his parentage, he noted with regret that his father "was always free from any desire of intellectual distinction on a large scale; I know that it was with reluctance that he preached at any time at Norwich, in London, or any other place where he suspected that his accents might fall on the ear of criticism." Godwin admits that his father "was something better than a merely learned man can ever be; he was a man of a warm heart and unblemished manners, ardent in his friendships. . . . He was extremely affectionate . . ." But what could all this mean to an ambitious lad who wryly recognized that, "at least to me, who was perhaps never his favourite, his rebukes had a painful tone of ill humour and asperity." [2]

William, the seventh child of thirteen, a child "sent from home to be nourished by a hireling," yet recognized that his mother, "so long as her husband lived, was the qualifier and moderator of his austerities. Some of the villagers were impertinent enough to allege that she was too gay in her style of decorating her person. She was facetious, and had an ambition to be thought the teller of a good story, and an adept at hitting off a smart repartee. . . ." This was Godwin's estimate of his mother as a wife, one whom, clearly, he admired, and with whom he identified himself in his own desire to shine in public and to rise in the world. But, after his father's death, his mother "became considerably changed. She surrendered herself to the visionary hopes and tormenting fears of the methodistical sect, and her ordinary economy became teazingly parsimonious." [3]

Under the influence of Miss Godwin (afterwards Mrs. Sothren), a first cousin of his father, Godwin's earliest books were John Bunyan's *Pilgrim's Progress* and James Janeway's *Account of the Pious Deaths of Many Godly Children*. The youthful heroes of the latter volume stirred the boy deeply: "Their premature eminence, suited to my age and station, strongly excited my emulation. I felt as if I were willing to die with them, if I could with equal success engage the admiration of my friends and mankind." [4] This early craving for public esteem was later transformed into a passionate desire to do so great a service to all humanity that his name would be forever enrolled among the heroes and benefactors of mankind. And so the precocious child, who had determined at the age of eight to become a Dissenting minister, "preached sermons in the kitchen every Sunday afternoon, and at other times, mounted in a child's high chair, indifferent as to the matter of persons present at these exhibitions, and undisturbed at their coming and going." [5]

The sense of destiny and uniquely personal sanctity is revealed in two other anecdotes from his journal. At the age of eleven, Godwin was sent to Norwich to receive instruction from the Reverend Mr. Samuel Newton, a Calvinist preacher. After the fashion of the times, Newton began his pedagogy by a long exhortation followed automatically by a birching. The self-anointed boy-prophet "listened at first with astonishment, and afterwards with incredulity. It had never occurred to me as possible that my person, which hitherto had been treated by most of my acquaintances, and particularly by Mrs. Sothren and Mr. Akers, who had principally engaged my attention, as something extraordinary and sacred, could suffer such ignominious violation. The idea had something in it as abrupt as a fall from heaven to earth. I had regarded this engine as the appropriate lot of the very refuse of the scholastic train." [6]

The other revealing incident has the texture of a dream recalled after long forgetfulness.

When I was about thirteen or fourteen years of age I went by myself one day at the period of the assizes to the Sessions House. Having gone early, I had my choice of a seat, and placed myself immediately next the bench. The judge was Lord Chief-Justice De Grey, afterwards Baron Walsingham. As I stayed some hours, I at one time relieved my posture by leaning my elbow on the corner of the cushion placed before his lordship. On some occasion, probably when he was going to address the jury, he laid his hand gently on my elbow and removed it. On this action I recollect having silently remarked, if his lordship knew what the lad beside him will perhaps one day become I am not sure that he would have removed my elbow." [7]

From such a childhood Godwin came to the writing of books for children—enforced from the outside by his radical notoriety that made it impossible to sign his own name to his works, but induced from within by a keen and life-long recognition of the crucial importance of childhood. John Middleton Murry describes him as a social martyr doing penance for his unreconstructed radicalism: "He had, without a murmur, given up writing the only sort of books that interested him to write—the books in which, as Hazlitt said, 'he gave himself,' and drudged for twenty years publishing books for children, in the vain hope of establishing some security for his family." [8]

But Godwin was also a writer of children's books with five children in his house: "Fanny, daughter of Mr. Imlay, who bears my own name, Mary, my own daughter by the same mother, two children of my present wife by a former husband, and a son, the offspring of my present marriage." [9] Murry recognizes that Godwin felt a real love for children for their own sakes, and it was that love that inspired his works about the education and rearing of children. His own children adored him and remained remarkably loyal to him through all his chequered career. When the wave of public reaction forced him to abandon political pamphleteering, he turned from the task of educating parents to the more important one of educating children through the interpretation of history. Because he considered children worthy of infinitely careful attention and analysis, he could write: "When the destination that is given to a child has been founded on a careful investigation of the faculties, tokens, and accidental aspirations which characterize his early years, it is then that every step that is made with him becomes a new and surer source of satisfaction." [10]

In *The History of England, for the Use of Schools and Young Persons,* written under the pseudonym of Edward Baldwin, Esquire, Godwin likened his method of composition to Molière's:

Molière, when he wrote his admirable comedies, was accustomed to read them in manuscript to an old woman, his housekeeper, and he always found that, where the old woman laughed or was out of humour, there the audience laughed or were out of humour also. In the same manner I am accustomed to consult my children in this humble species of writing in which I have engaged. I put the two or three first sections of this work into their hands as a specimen. Their remark was How easy this is! Why we learn it by heart, almost as fast as we read it! Their suffrage gave me courage, and I carried on my work to the end.[11]

This same interest and concern for the proper development of children—and perhaps his own recollection of the Reverend Mr. Newton and his cane—made him critical of the tyrannical schoolmaster of the period: "In the little world of the classroom, teacher and pupil are not to assume the parts of tyrant and slave: the child's natural dignity and candour are precious and ought not to be undermined . . . a 'uniform, even tenour of conduct' should be maintained, and the 'gentle yoke of the preceptor should be confounded as much as possible, with the eternal laws of nature and necessity. There is not in the world a truer object of pity than a child terrified at every glance, and watching, with anxious uncertainty, the caprices of a pedagogue.'" [12]

With the objectivity of a friend of children, he is able to see that the most important influences may not come from the book or the lecture or the classroom exercise, but from the experience of learning to live together with other youths: "It is when the schoolboy proceeds to the playground that he engages in real action and real discussion: it is then that he is an absolute human being and a genuine individual." [13] A man is the product of all he has experienced, and education is part of that shaping whole. But education can be used as a powerful instrument of conformity, and the most ductile student may have had all creativity, initiative, and individuality drained out of him by the educative process. Instead of the creation of a mob of automata—obedient slaves of the "positive institutions" of church and state—Godwin aims at the development of free individuals who will be absolutely human and genuinely individual. On March 2, 1802, William Godwin wrote to William Cole about this very primacy of the personal development of the individual child:

". . . I am most peremptorily of opinion against putting children extremely forward. If they desire to themselves, I would not baulk them, for I love to attend to these unsophisticated indications. But otherwise, *Festina lente* is my maxim in education. I think the worst consequences flow from overloading the faculties of children, and a forced maturity. We should always remember that the object of education is the future man or woman; and it is a miserable vanity that would sacrifice the wholesome and gradual development of the mind to the desire of exhibiting little monsters of curiosity." [14]

Against the record of Godwin's indebtedness to Shelley and to the many other victims of his importunity, and the resulting epithet of "Venerable horseleech" which was applied to him by Sir Leslie Stephen in his life of Godwin for the *Dictionary of Na-*

tional Biography, it is necessary to set the equally factual record of the tireless energy and high gallantry of spirit which kept him fighting against a wave of pauperism that, despite his very best efforts, was continually threatening to drown his family, during the last twenty-five years of his life. Furthermore, during this period of strenuous industry and perpetual bankruptcy, he offered lodging, understanding, and monetary help to the long list of young disciples already mentioned in Chapter III. And along with that concern for the young who sought him out, there was the larger compassion for childhood everywhere victimized, intimidated, and deformed—often for the best of reasons by the most high-minded of mistaken zealots.

Thus Godwin's novels, with their revelation of the political philosopher's realm of feeling, abound with children warped and twisted by false ideals of education. There is Barnabas Tyrrel (*Caleb Williams*), whose undisciplined childhood has created a rural bully. In the same novel, Ferdinando Falkland is the victim of a chivalric honor and personal pride which came to him through the corrupting influence of tales and verse. St. Leon early inbibed the same ideals of chivalry and honor as Falkland, and like him was poisoned by them. Fleetwood was the lonely child of a melancholy father, shocked by the school follies of young roughs at Oxford, and embittered by the coquetry of French ladies of fashion. Mandeville received a traumatic wound from witnessing, at the age of three, the massacre of his parents. For eight years, he was exposed to the baleful influences of a melancholy uncle and a gloomy and depressing mansion. His twisted fate was further sealed by a boyhood enthusiasm for the world of chivalry which blossomed in his early manhood into a life-long allegiance to the cause of Charles Stuart. Cloudesley had an idyllic youth which led him to imagine that all of his life would continue in the same vein. The naïve idealism of his youth, which was inadequate preparation for the unidyllic reality of life, was twisted into misanthropy by an unjust prison sentence, making him the perfect tool for the sinister designs of his employer. Deloraine is the usual victim of false ideals of personal honor just as Travers, his avenging pursuer, is the victim of his father's unrewarded philanthropy. These full-length novelistic studies of warped childhood can be ampli-

fied by the searing indignation of his description in *Fleetwood* of
the children who work in the silk factories of Lyons.

An Account of the Seminary . . . For the Instruction of Twelve Pupils, *1783*

The author who was so keenly interested in children began his
career by almost becoming a schoolmaster, and at the middle of
that career he settled down to the writing of books for school
children. In 1783, Godwin prepared a prospectus for a small
school he proposed to start at Epsom in Surrey. The brief advertisement bore the lengthy title *An Account of the Seminary that
will be opened on Monday the Fourth Day of August, at Epsom
in Surrey, for the Instruction of Twelve Pupils in the Greek, Latin,
French, and English Languages.* The goal was modest enough,
but the twelve pupils were never obtained; the school became
a mere prospectus, and the would-be schoolmaster returned to
preaching, journalism, and finally to his lifework as a writer.

Fables Ancient and Modern, *1805*

Twenty-two years later, Godwin wrote *Fables Ancient and
Modern,* the first of his volumes for children, under the pseudonym Edward Baldwin. His doctrinaire turn of mind is immediately apparent in the Preface when he laments the statement of a
fable in five or six lines: "A tale which is compressed, dry and
told in as few words as a problem in Euclid, will never prove
interesting to the mind of a child . . . . we must expatiate upon
some points; we must introduce quick, unexpected turns, which, if
they are not wit, have the effect of wit to children. Above all, we
must make our narrations pictures, and render the objects we discourse about visible to the fancy of the learner." Thus the basic
technique of Baldwin's fables is revealed as the retelling of familiar, brief stories in expanded and dramatic storytelling form.

But the fables are to be moral, as well, for Godwin observes
that "Half the Fables which are to be found in the ordinary books
end unhappily, or end in an abrupt and unsatisfactory manner.
This is what a child does not like. The first question he asks, when
he has finished his reading, if he is at all interested in the tale, is
What became of the poor dog, the fox, or the wolf? While the

stories were told with the customary dryness this was not of much importance; but, the moment a character of reality was given to the narrative"—by Godwin's revisions—"it cried aloud for correction. I have accordingly endeavoured to make almost all my narratives end in a happy and forgiving tone, in that tone of mind which I would wish to cultivate in my child." [15] Godwin seems unaware that the expansion of a fable, the motivation of character, and the moralizing of endings has quite transformed the fable into a story of a very different sort.

The fables, written between February 22 and March 26, were published in October, 1805. They marked the beginning of a new literary venture in which Mr. and Mrs. Godwin determined to make a living out of literature—he, by writing under the necessary pseudonym; she, by doing the bulk of the translations and carrying on the business. Of the books thus produced, the work that will live (requested by Godwin and published by his wife) is *Tales from Shakespeare* by Charles and Mary Lamb. Also of merit is Godwin's revision and abridgement of Hazlitt's grammar, which was widely used. But the twenty years during which the business was carried on were one long story of struggle, industry, ingenuity, and failure. [16]

The History of England, for the Use of Schools and Young Persons, *1806*

Encouraged by the reception of his fables, Godwin set to work to apply to history the reverse technique. He noted in the Preface to *The History of England* that most history books were too long and too detailed; moreover, they were written in a dry, repulsive style. He determined that his pages would not be "crowded with a variety of articles; they are so printed as to be agreeable and refreshing to the eye of a child. I wished to give him a bird's eye view of the History of England, not to exhibit it by the aid of a microscope. For this reason I seldom or ever found it necessary to take down a book from my shelf as I wrote. I had nothing to do but with the great landmarks of history which can never be obliterated."

He explained to the parents of his prospective readers his criterion for use or omission of a fact or a date: "I hold that those particulars of which an accomplished gentleman and a scholar may without dishonour confess that he has no recollection, are a superfluity with which it is quite unnecessary to load the memory of a child . . ." And so with his own little domestic group placed in a circle about him, he tried out the pages of his text, reading aloud, dramatizing, relating, questioning, and encouraging competition in the learning process.

The History of Greece, *1811*

When William Godwin was a student in the home of the Reverend Mr. Newton, he was free to read at will in his master's library. The books that meant most to him were "the early volumes of the English translation of the *Ancient History* of Rollin. Few bosoms ever beat with greater ardour than mine did while perusing the story of the grand struggle of the Greeks for independence against the assaults of the Persian despot; and this scene awakened a passion in my soul which will never cease but with life." [17]

It is a mistake to refuse to recognize that this passion in the soul bore two literary fruits. The one which all would acknowledge is the mighty *Political Justice*, which was in its way, a "grand struggle . . . for independence." The other fruitage was the simple, sincere retelling of part of that ancient history in *The History of Greece*, published in 1811 "by Edward Baldwin." Perhaps some other lad would have a passion for freedom kindled in his soul by reading the history book, and as a man, shape that passion with the reading of the book of political philosophy.

When Godwin and his wife went into the business of publishing books for children, he was almost fifty years old and had to adopt such pseudonyms as Edward Baldwin and Theophilus Marcliffe, because of the public notoriety of his real name. Besides the works already mentioned, the busy house on Skinner Street published children's histories of Rome, *The Pantheon, or Ancient History of the Gods of Greece and Rome*, *The Looking Glass*, and Lamb's *Adventures of Ulysses*.

II *History for Adults*
The History of the Life of William Pitt, Earl of Chatham, *1783*

Godwin left his pastorate at Stowmarket in April, 1782, because of a dispute with the elders of his congregation over a question concerning church discipline—a question which he never specifically designated. His faith in Christianity had already been shaken by some books shared with him by a Mr. Norman, and so he was somewhat relieved to have a specific cause for severing a connection that was steadily becoming more and more distressing. Fawcet and some other friends who were accustomed to drop in at his meager lodging in Holborn persuaded Godwin to try writing. First, he drew up another prospectus, not now for an abortive academy but for an equally unfecund series of English biographies for periodical publication. He began with an article on William Pitt, Earl of Chatham, supposedly of a length appropriate for periodical publication; but, in a fashion that became characteristic of his works, the article grew beneath his pen until, instead of part of a series, he had a book, but not a particularly good one. He characterized it himself as "a very wretched attempt." Perhaps this evaluation explains his return for the first seven months of 1783 to Beaconsfield, once more as a Dissenting pastor. But, after this brief refresher in the trials of the pastorate, he returned to the industrious production of a play, several novels, a collection of sermons, and finally any literary odd job he could find that would amplify his slender income—pamphleteering, translating, indexing, and ghost writing for political figures.

The industry of this period, and indeed of all periods of his literary life, is described by his daughter.

"He rose, between seven and eight, and read some classic author before breakfast. From nine till twelve or one he occupied himself with his pen. He found that he could not exceed this measure of labour with any advantage to his own health, or the work in hand . . . the rest of the morning was spent in reading and seeing his friends. When at home he dined at four, but during his bachelor life he frequently dined out. His dinner at home at this time was simple enough. He had no regular servant; an old woman came in the morning to clean and arrange his rooms, and if necessary she prepared a mutton chop, which was put in a Dutch oven." [18]

But the first fruits of all this industry were so embarrassing to the author, that Hazlitt later gibed, no doubt effectively, "The world do not know (and we are not sure but the intelligence may startle Mr. Godwin himself), that he is the author of a volume of Sermons, and of a life of Chatham." [19]

The Life of Geoffrey Chaucer, *1803*

For Godwin's *Life of Chaucer* Hazlitt had no gibes, only praise: "His *Life of Chaucer* would have given celebrity to any man of letters possessed of three thousand a year, with leisure to write quartos. . . ." [20] The work was published in four volumes with the magniloquent title *The Life of Geoffrey Chaucer, the Early English Poet: including Memoirs of His Near Friend and Kinsman, John of Gaunt, Duke of Lancaster; with Sketches of the Manners, Opinions, Arts and Literature of England in the Fourteenth Century.*

Chapters I-XIII of this book trace the life of Chaucer from his birth through his education at Cambridge; Chapter XIV follows him to Oxford; Chapter XVIII raises the questions whether Chaucer studied at Paris and was enrolled in the Inner Temple; in Chapter XIX he enters the service of Edward III and in Chapter XXIII he participates in the grand invasion of France. In Chapter XXVII there is the account of his first pension and in Chapter XXIX of his marriage. Chapter XXXV finds Chaucer in Italy and recounts his interview with Petrarch; in Chapter XXXVI he receives a grant of a pitcher of wine *per diem* for life and is appointed comptroller of the customs; in Chapter XXXVIII he obtains the wardship of Edmund Stapelgate; in Chapter XL he is part of an embassy to France; in Chapter XLIX he is involved in the contention over the mayoralty of London; in Chapter L Chaucer, in exile, is financially embarrassed, returns to England and is imprisoned in the Tower of London. Upon his release, he is deprived of his appointments and sells his pensions, as well as impeaching his former associates. Chapter LI notes Chaucer's appointment as clerk of works and his resignation after the return of John of Gaunt, and his subsequent retirement to Woodstock, when he receives a pension of twenty pounds per annum. In Chapter LII Chaucer moves to Donnington and re-engages in public affairs; he receives a patent of protection and a grant of wine. In Chapter LIII Henry Bolingbroke is banished, John of Gaunt dies, and Chaucer moves to London, in high favor with the new sovereign, Richard II. Chapter LIV recounts the death of Chaucer, and Chapter LV considers his character.

One of the strong values of the work is the analysis of the characteristics of the period, as indicated by part of the title: "with Sketches of the Manners, Opinions, Arts and Literature of England in the Fourteenth Century." Godwin describes London in the fourteenth century, the state of learning in England under the Norman and Plantagenet princes, romance and its connection with the feudal system, the establishment and practices of the English church, the diversions of our ancestors, architecture, sculpture and painting, the state of education at Cambridge and Oxford, a history of the development of poetry, a full consideration of the political life of the period, and a lengthy analysis of the teachings of Wycliffe and the Lollards. Godwin recognized the importance to understanding of a poet of reference to the age in which he lived, and he hoped that his work on Chaucer might encourage other Englishmen to master the vernacular of late Middle English, which seemed to him as important as the study of Greek and Latin.

Godwin as a literary critic places the talent of Chaucer just below the gifts of Shakespeare. Of the *Canterbury Tales*, he notes that "splendour of narrative, richness of fancy, pathetic simplicity of incident and feeling, a powerful style in delineating character and manners, and an animated vein of comic humour, each takes its turn in this wonderful performance, and each in turn appears to be that in which the author was most qualified to excell." [21] As a literary innovator, "Chaucer fixed and naturalized the genuine art of poetry in our island. But what is most memorable in his eulogy, is that he is the father of our language, the idiom of which was by the Norman conquest banished from courts and civilized life, and which Chaucer was the first to restore to literature, and the muses." [22] Later in the book, Godwin points out:

Mandeville, Wicliffe and Gower, whom we may style the other three evangelists of our tongue, though all elder in birth than Chaucer, did not begin so early to work upon the ore of their native language. He surprised his countrymen with a poem, eminently idiomatic, clear and perspicuous in its style, as well as rich and harmonious in its versification. His *Court of Love*, an earlier production, is not less excellent in both these respects. But it was too slight and short to awaken general attention. The *Troilus and Creseide* was of respectable magnitude, and forms an epoch in our literature. . . . He presents real life and human sentiments, and suffers the reader to dwell upon and expand the operations of feeling and passion.[23]

However, Godwin's critical talents recognized both Chaucer's virtues and his faults: "To judge from the poem *Troilus and Creseide*, we should be tempted to say that compression, the strengthening of a sentiment by brevity, and the adding to the weight and power of a work by cutting away from it all useless and cumbersome excrescences, was a means of attaining to excellence which never entered into our author's mind." [24]

Though a Dissenting clergyman, Godwin appreciates the interpenetration of art and worship in the Roman Catholic faith and the contribution thus made to Chaucer's time:

The authors or improvers of the Romish religion were perfectly aware of the influence which the senses possess over the heart and the character. The buildings which they constructed for the purposes of public worship are exquisitely venerable. Their stained and painted windows admit only a "dim, religious light." The magnificence of the fabric, its lofty and concave roof, the massy pillars, the extensive ailes, and the splendid choirs, are all calculated to inspire the mind with religious solemnity. Music, paintings, images, decoration, nothing is omitted which may fill the soul with devotion. The uniform garb of the monks and nuns, their decent gestures, and the slowness of their procession cannot but call off the most frivolous mind from the concern of ordinary life. The solemn chaunt and the sublime anthem must compose and elevate the heart. The splendour of the altar, the brilliancy of the tapers, the smoke and fragrance of the incense, and the sacrifice, as is pretended, of God himself, make every celebration of public worship an occasion of solemnity.[25]

Despite the general atmosphere of positive appreciation, Godwin's use of "calculated" and the gratuitous insult of "as is pretended" bear the marks of the forensics of the Dissenting chapel.

Surprising, also, are his estimates of feudalism and Lollardism. Godwin claims that "It is principally to the feudal system that we owe the distinguishing features of modern, as contrasted with ancient Europe, that we belong more to our families and less to the state, that we are more of men and less of machines. The great chain of subordination in the feudal law, had generated among and entailed upon us a continual respect to the combinations and affections which bind man to man, and neighbour to neighbour. . . ." Perhaps even more paradoxically, the creator of Falkland, St. Leon, Mandeville, Lord Alton, and Deloraine—all destroyed by false senses of honor arising from a youthful exposure to chivalry and romance—calls "The feudal system . . . the nurse of chivalry, and the parent of romance; and out of these have sprung the principle of modern honour in the best sense of that term, the generosity of disinterested adventure, and the more persevering and successful cultivation of the private affections." [26]

In general, Godwin approved of Wycliffe's attack on the religious abuses of his day, but he feels constrained to point out to his readers that Wycliffe's belief was similar to that of Calvin— gloomy, revolting to the understanding and the heart—and that sympathizers with the persecuted Lollards must remember that Wycliffe and his followers were themselves narrow and savagely intolerant bigots. The Peasant Revolt, while an expression of the spirit that questions the despotic authority of the church and the state, was, in Godwin's opinion, a prime example of that violent and premature anarchism which he had deplored in *Political Justice*. Another echo of this great work is his excoriation of war as "the most humiliating attitude in which human nature can exhibit itself. A thousand men murdered on a field, by other men to whom they are total strangers, for a miserable question of political speculation, by which, ninety-nine times out of a hundred, whichever party obtains the victory, no party is the gainer, is a spectacle to make us curse existence, and the human form we bear." [27] His high aim was

to produce a work of a new species. Antiquities have too generally been regarded as the province of men of cold tempers and sterile imaginations, writers who, by their phlegmatic and desultory industry, have brought discredit upon a science, which is perhaps beyond all others fraught with wisdom, moral instruction and intellectual improvement. . . . It was my wish, had my power held equal pace with my strong inclination, to carry the workings of fancy and the spirit of philosophy into the investigation of ages past. I was anxious to rescue for a moment the illustrious dead from the jaws of the grave, to make them pass in review before me, to question their spirits and record their answers.[28]

[134]

Lives of Edward and John Philips, Nephews and Pupils of Milton, *1809*

"The two persons who constitute the subject of the present volume were nephews of Milton, were brought up under his roof, and in some measure adopted by him as his sons. Their history . . . affords us an advantage in studying his character, which it rarely happens for the admirers of a great genius or a poet to possess." [29] Thus Godwin, in the Preface, indicated his approach to a study of Milton, an approach further delineated by the full title: *Lives of Edward and John Philips, Nephews and Pupils of Milton, Including Various Particulars of the Literary and Political History of Their Times, to Which are added, 1. "Collections for the Life of Milton," by John Aubrey, Printed from the Manuscript Copy in the Ashmolean Museum at Oxford, 2. "The Life of Milton" by Edward Philips, printed in the year 1694.*

Ann Milton, the mother of Edward and John Philips, was John Milton's only sister and probably several years older than the poet, for one of her children died in infancy in 1625, when John was seventeen years of age. It was the death of this child that occasioned one of Milton's earliest poems in English, "On the Death of a fair Infant dying of a Cough." Ann's first husband, Edward Philips, died in 1631. Some time later Ann married a Mr. Thomas Agar, by whom she had two daughters, Mary, who died young, and Ann, who was still alive when Edward Philips (Jr.) published his *Life of Milton* (1694). When John Milton returned from his Continental travels, he assumed responsibility for his sister's two sons by her first marriage, John aged nine, and Edward, one year older. He took John as soon as he had found lodgings in St. Bride's Church Yard. When he moved to a pretty garden house in Aldersgate Street, Edward joined them, and the young bachelor uncle undertook the education of his nephews according to his own theories of education.

About Milton's own marriage much has been written and more conjectured. But Godwin contented himself with a quotation from Edward Philips' *Life of Milton:* " 'About Whitsuntide it was, or a little after, that he took a journey into the country; nobody about him certainly knowing the reason, or that it was any more than a journey of recreation: after a month's stay, home he returns a married man, that went out a bachelor.'" [30] The unhappy marriage flowered in Milton's tracts on marriage and divorce, particularly in *The Doctrine and Discipline of Divorce* and *Tetrachordon, or an Exposition of the Four Chief Places in Scripture, which treat of Marriage, or Nullities in Marriage*. Milton examines the Scripture on marriage and divorce in a very peculiar way. He notes that the law of Moses sanctions divorce for "*incompatibility of temper*" but that Jesus pronounces that "whosoever shall put away his wife except it be for fornication, and shall marry another, committeth adultery." Milton, out of his own unfortunate domestic situation, as well as his sensitivity to the problem of living intimately with a mismatched mate, argues that what Moses said should be taken for law; what Christ said, for advice. He reminds the reader that Christ, at the beginning of the Sermon on the Mount, assured men that he "came not to destroy the law"— that is, the law of Moses. Therefore, the law of Moses is still in force among Christians. At the same time, Christ's Kingdom was "not of this world"; therefore, the king of that kingdom could scarcely originate civil or canon laws. It is obvious that Milton's point of view on this matter would be particularly attractive to Godwin, with his insistence on individual liberty and on the harm positive institutions do to human life whenever they abridge that liberty.

At the beginning of Milton's career, the Puritan cause seemed entirely certain of success. But when Presbyterian elders became as tyrannical as Romish priests, and the Independents began squabbling among themselves, the restoration of the Stuart line became a real possibility. At that point, when Milton was anxiously watching the "signs of the times," his own nephews went over to the enemy and became staunch Royalists. Godwin leaves us in no doubt concerning his own attitude toward the Stuarts:

The most resplendent period of the English nation, was that, at which this family came out from the remoter north, to occupy the throne of these kingdoms. Great were we at that time in arts and arms. Never did genius and invention, all that is profound in research, or rich and commanding in language, or capacious and magnificent in poetry, so much abound among us. This was the age of grave and honourable manners, and of real politicians and statesmen. We could then boast of a Raleigh and a Bacon, of Coke, of Grenville, of Selden, of Sackville, of Shakespeare, of Jonson, of Fletcher, or Drayton, and many more, examples of what Englishmen were, and hostages and assurances, in appearance, of what they would be. But it pleased heaven to give a different event. The island was successively plagued with a sceptred pedant in the first place, a wretch of coward heart and groveling dispositions, inspiring no man with awe, and cherishing no man with willingness, but such as were only distinguished by personal beauty, presumptuous aims, and insolent manners. Then came a sober, cold-blooded, ungracious successor, a lover of despotism as his father was, and of a saturnine temper to render the propensity more formidable in his breast. His sons have been sufficiently described; the elder remorseless, with an impudence of profligacy, political and personal, unknown to modern times; and the younger, still less human in his dispositions, with super-added to this, a fixed resolution to impose upon his country an unmitigated slavery, both civil and religious.

But here a distinction is to be made. The evils that occurred under the first two of these princes were not unattended with salutary consequences, and impressed the people of England with a deeper feeling of the value of liberty, than they might ever have learned under a more auspicious government. But the Restoration was an event of unmitigated calamity. The character of the English nation at this time became retrograde; and though the expulsion of the Stuart family to a certain degree reduced the disease, yet it is probable that the nation has never recovered that tone of independence, strong thinking, and generosity, which the Restoration so powerfully operated to destroy.[31]

Although Edward and John Philips had taken the opposite political side from their uncle, Godwin suggests the possibility that Edward, at least, may have been instrumental in obtaining Milton's indemnity from the Restoration government. Sir Thomas Clarges, brother-in-law of General Monk, was the courtier who helped to protect the Puritan poet. He is also the person whose private papers were turned over to Edward Philips for some literary compilation. "May we not indulge a hope then," asks Godwin, "that this young man was fortunate enough to have been an active instrument, in securing the safety and life of the author of *Paradise Lost?*" [32] Godwin seems to feel sure that John Philips, on the other hand, "as long as he existed never relaxed in his unnatural animosity to Milton. . . ." [33]

The political differences between Milton and his nephews pose a particular problem to Godwin that they do not present to us. If a person is born without innate characteristics, and becomes the product of all the sense impressions that bombard his developing personality from the outside world, how did it happen that the nephews of a great and good man should be so extremely different from the very person who was unquestionably one of the strongly influential forces upon their development? Godwin's answer suggests the arguer himself was only half-convinced by his argument:

It would scarcely be right to close the volume upon the lives of these two brothers, without moralizing a little on their case, one of the most striking and conclusive that ever occurred, of a trial of what I may call the antagonist powers of nature and education. . . . Yet the nephews of the great poet threw off the peculiar and favourite modes of thinking of their uncle, by the time they were twenty-four or twenty-five years of age; I know not how much sooner. How are we to account for this? It was not that their understandings rejected his reasonings, and that as they grew up, they entered into a more just and a wider field of observation; it was the weakness and unmanliness of their tempers, that corrupted their heart, and obscured their judgment. They associated with what Edward Philips calls in his *History* "the jovial cavaliers." It was not probably a cold calculation of interest that at first seduced them. There was little probability in 1655 that the old government would ever be restored. But they liked the careless jollity and merriment of the royalists; and this point being gained, their calculations then leaned to the side of their wishes, and in the midst of songs, and jests, and intemperate revelry, they learned to doubt no longer that "the king would have his own again." [34]

The embarrassment of the philosophical moralist is apparent when we realize that reason ought to have given its persuasive witness to the truth of Milton's position; hence, the difficulty must be with something in the nephews' natures. But their natures were formed under Milton's nurture, so we have to posit a basic lowness of nature and a strong attractiveness of error among "the jovial cavaliers." Thus what living with Milton could not do was accomplished easily by "songs, and jests, and intemperate revelry."

Because of the friendly relationship of Edward and John with Titus Oates, Godwin is drawn into discussion of the whole unsavory legal mess. When Godwin read John Philips' pamphlet defending his friend, he indignantly remounted his deserted pulpit:

Oates, by his atrocious proceedings, his calm and undaunted perjuries, destroyed twenty innocent men by the hands of the executioner, and twice as many in the darkness and miseries of a prison, filled the whole island with frantic alarms by his incredible lies, and brought a disgrace on the nation itself which I am afraid can hardly be paralleled in systematic and deliberate injustice, in the history of any other age or country: and John Philips writes his pamphlet, in virtuous terror lest his beloved friend Titus Oates, by the "scurrilous and treasonable libels" published against him, should be bereaved of the opportunity of committing more murders.[35]

Godwin's consideration of the Titus Oates trials leads him to his favorite irritation concerning the attitude of judges toward the accused. In *Political Justice* he had done his best to restore the judicial function to its rightful sphere and to defend the rights and independence of the accused. Now in his work on Milton and his nephews, he returns powerfully to the same theme:

Nothing can be more odious to a liberal mind, than the practice which unhappily takes place in some degree in all courts of justice, of measuring the words of the persons arraigned before them, and requiring them to speak in what is called, "the manner befitting their unhappy situation." The insolence of the judges, the delight they apparently feel in interrupting, in checking, in rebuking and trampling upon the prisoners brought before them, which we more or less perceive in the reading of all trials, certainly conduces to none of the ends of justice. They expect to be emphatically thanked for their generosity, if they practice any degree of decency towards the man whose cause they are appointed to hear, and if they consent to put him to death with any sort of gentility. They look for a canting and hypocritical profession of offence and of sorrow, and hold out a lure, often a fallacious one, that such profession shall be considered in mitigation of punishment. They are more anxious to degrade and to dishonour, than to inflict the censure of the law. If a man fairly asserts his own conception of his case, and refuses to acknowledge offence, where, whatever may be the judgment of the ministers of the law, he finds none, this is treated as a heinous aggravation of his legal guilt; and many a one has paid the forfeit of his life, merely because he has spoken upon his trial that firm language, which is calculated to honour his memory to the latest posterity.

The very reverse of this ought to be the case. It is a maxim of equity in the most ordinary walks of life, that losers have a privilege to talk. It is a very small boon that is granted me, if when I am ready to abide all that you can inflict upon me, I be permitted quietly and without interruption to express my own sense of my own action. Nothing can be more iniquitous, than to take any thing I shall there say, into the consideration of what punishment I shall sustain. I am tried for a certain imputed offence; that offence is, or ought to be contained precisely in my indictment; and you have no more right to punish me, for any thing I have done since the time to which the indictment refers, than for the assassination of Servius Tullius, king of Rome. What I require is, as one of our poets expresses it, that I may

'have room
To entertain my fate, and die with decency.'

and what I would say is, If I am to die, allow me to act the last scene of my life with honour; and if I am to live do not require me to purchase a few added years of infirm and declining life with the words or the gestures of a poltroon.[36]

Along with these weightier matters of the law, an interesting little literary feud develops between Dr. Samuel Johnson and William Godwin. At the time of John Milton's death and burial, a work was published by his nephew Edward Philips, entitled *Theatrum Poetarum, or a Compleat Collection of the Poets, especially the most Eminent, of all Ages.* In his discussion of the work, Godwin comments that "Dr. Johnson, whose neglect of all the sources of information, can only be equalled by the dogmaticalness of his assertions, having occasion to mention it in his *Lives of the Poets,* says, 'From this wonder-working academe [Milton's plan for the education of his nephews, in conjunction with the sons of some gentlemen, his friends], I do not know that there ever proceeded any man very eminent for knowledge: its only genuine product I believe is a small *History of Poetry,* written in Latin by his nephew Philips, of which perhaps none of my readers has ever heard.' "

Godwin considers that "It is not easy . . . in all the annals of literature, to parallel the insolence and ignorance of this paragraph." Then he proceeds to demolish Dr. Johnson's critical judgment in four arguments. First, just a few pages later in the *Lives of the Poets,* Dr. Johnson refers to John Philips' *Responsio ad Apolo-*

giam cujusdam Anonymi, thus proving that he knew of at least one other product of Milton's "wonder-working academy." Second, Dr. Johnson had himself referred to Edward Philips' biography of his uncle for his own life of Milton. Third, although it is evident that Johnson never read the *Theatrum Poetarum*—he describes it as "written in Latin" and only the first two words of the title are in Latin—he must have noted in books by Jacob and Cibber that their references to primary sources were frequently in the form of quotations from Philips and Winstanley. Fourth, at any time Dr. Johnson cared to consult literary authorities he could have found a list of the complete writings of the Philips brothers in Winstanley, Wood, Jacob, and in the *Theatrum Poetarum* itself. Godwin, with his careful research technique, evidently could not bear "Dr. Johnson's confident way of talking in the midst of the deepest ignorance." [37]

History of the Commonwealth of England, 1824-1828

The waspish pen of William Hazlitt described his contemporary Godwin as a man who, "In common company . . . either goes to sleep himself, or sets others to sleep. He is at present engaged in a History of the Commonwealth of England.—*Esto Perpetua!*" [38] Everlasting or not, it was another example of the way Godwin's "hack work" often blossomed into large works of loving literary labor. Writing to Mary Shelley he exulted, "In my seventy-second year I am all cheerfulness, and never anticipate the evil day till to do so is absolutely unavoidable . . . my present cheerfulness is greatly owing to Cromwell, and the nature of my occupation, which gives me an object *omnium horarum,* a stream for ever running and for ever new." [39]

From quite different points of view both Hazlitt and Godwin seem to have been thinking about "forever" in connection with the *History of the Commonwealth of England.* At any rate Godwin's growing fascination with his subject had overcome any of the reluctant sense of writing for bread, and had produced a vigorous, able, and generally scholarly study of a misunderstood and maligned period in British history. The last volume, wholly devoted to a full-length portrait of Oliver Cromwell, deserves comparison with Carlyle's great study. Godwin recognizes that only an extraordinary man could struggle against all the parties, religious and political, in his realm; subdue all of them; unite England; and raise her international prowess to a point unknown before. He gives full attention to the political and military genius of the man. But perhaps Godwin's great contribution to the understanding of Cromwell comes out of his own experience. He was a Dissenter writing about a Dissenter, an Independent interpreting an Independent. He had shared the Protestant dream of the Heavenly Kingdom, and in *Political Justice* he had attempted to translate it into political, moral, and economic terms. He was eminently equipped to comprehend Cromwell's effort to transform England into something resembling the millennial rule of the Saints.

As the biography's motto from Burke suggested,—"to attend to the neglected, and to remember the forgotten"—Godwin realized that he had to resurrect not only a man but a reputation, not only a political leader, but a political epoch and its philosophy of government. He became the champion of those parliamentary leaders who brought the Commonwealth into being. He saw all the acts of Parliament, up to the establishment of the Commonwealth, as worthy in themselves or necessary to the inauguration of a glorious era. The tragic shadow over the book is cast by the figure of Cromwell, who is meant to be the avenging and reigning angel of God's sovereignty, but who, like Milton's Satan, fell because of "unhallowed ambition." His desertion from the cause of parliamentary government destroyed it. His dissolution of the Rump Parliament in 1653 was the single, unredeemable act which spelled the ruin of the Commonwealth: "He taught his countrymen to be incredulous to the name of public liberty. He prepared the way for all . . . the infamy of the reign of Charles the Second." [40]

Lives of the Necromancers, *1834*

In 1834, Godwin published that curious work, *Lives of the Necromancers: or An Account of the Most Eminent Persons in Successive Ages, Who have Claimed for Themselves, or to Whom has Been Imputed by Others, the Exercise of Magical Power.* He begins his survey with an account of the superstitions of the ancient world, and ends it with the witch trials held in New England at the close of the seventeenth century. The great apostle of Reason states in the Preface that the main purpose of the book was "to

exhibit a fair delineation of the credulity of the human mind."
The clergyman-moralist feels that such an exhibition could not fail
to produce some excellent moral lessons.

The first lesson Godwin draws is a "useful pride in the abun-
dance of our faculties." It is pride that stimulates man to undertake
great things. If a man does not value himself highly, he will be of
little value. Would any man set to work to produce an important
work—whether imaginative, scientific, or intellectual—without
pride? But the most remarkable thing about man's capacity for
imagination and reason is his ability to take "to pieces the sub-
stances that are, and combine their parts into new arrangements."
Here Godwin speaks as the disciple of David Hartley, who postu-
lated all abstract ideas as combinations of simple sensory phenomena:

He [man] peoples all the elements from the world of his imagination.
It is here that he is most extraordinary and wonderful. The record of
what actually is, and has happened in the series of human events, is
perhaps the smallest part of human history. If we would know man in
all his subtleties, we must deviate into the world of miracles and sor-
cery. To know the things that are not, and cannot be, but have been
imagined and believed, is the most curious chapter in the annals of
man. To observe the actual results of these imaginary phenomena, and
the crimes and cruelties they have caused us to commit, is one of the
most instructive studies in which we can possibly be engaged. It is here
that man is most astonishing, and that we contemplate with most admiration the discursive and unbounded nature of his faculties.[41]

But, if a survey of man's ability to imagine what is not is conducive to pride, it is also conducive, reminds our moralist, of humility. The glory of man is his reason. It is the power to make inference and connection, to analyze and compare, to invent ingenious
machinery, and to discover the systematic nature both of the
physical universe and of moral philosophy. "Yet what so irrational
as man: Not contented with making use of the powers we possess,
for the purpose of conducing to our accommodation and well being, we with a daring spirit inquire into the invisible causes of
what we see, and people all nature with Gods 'of every shape and
size' and angels, with principalities and powers, with beneficent
beings who 'take charge concerning us lest at any time we dash

our foot against a stone,' and with devils who are perpetually on the watch to perplex us and do us injury. . . ." No sooner do we use the power of reason to understand the regularity and systematic working of the physical universe "than we frame to ourselves the idea, by the aid of some invisible ally, of suspending their operation, of calling out meteors in the sky, of commanding storms and tempests, of arresting the motion of heavenly bodies, of producing miraculous cures upon the bodies of our fellow-men, or afflicting them with disease and death, or calling up the deceased from the silence of the grave, and compelling them to disclose the secrets of the world unknown." [42] The most revealing and deplorable aspect of man's invocation of invisible deity is that he is not content with the aid of God and angels, but must also aspire to enter into alliance with Satan and devils—and this is a major theme in the history of necromancy.[43]

In his lengthy discussion of men who have claimed magical powers, Godwin found very few whom he would describe as charlatans, who with cool calculation set about the deception of their fellows. He seems to have considered the great majority self-deluded as well as delusive, and to have felt that they were themselves, in the final analysis, the most cruelly tricked by their unfounded superstitions. "One useful lesson which we may derive from the detail of these particulars, is the folly in most cases of imputing pure and unmingled hypocrisy to man. The human mind is of so ductile a character that, like what is affirmed of charity by the apostle, it 'believeth all things, and endureth all things.' We are not at liberty to trifle with the sacredness of truth. While we persuade others, we begin to deceive ourselves." [44]

The final moral of the work was the importance of a rational view of the universe: "let us . . . hail with heart-felt gladness the light which has, though late, broken in upon us, and weep over the calamity of our forefathers, who in addition to the inevitable ills of our sublunary state, were harassed with imaginary terrors. . . ." [45]

CHAPTER 6

Conclusion

SOME of the vituperation of Godwin's contemporaries, plus the condemnation of the Shelley-Mary Godwin relationship, carries over into the modern critical estimate of Godwin. As recently as 1950, D. C. Somervell wrote, in *English Thought in the Nineteenth Century*, "Godwin is one of those philosophical gasbags who has been so long pricked and deflated that it is extremely difficult to reconstruct him in the dimensions he assumed in the eyes of his contemporaries." [1] But in 1956 Russell Noyes reminds us that "more than a century after his death students of political theory still turn with inquiring minds to the writings of the philosopher described by Herbert Read as 'the first and most eloquent prophet of libertarian socialism.' " [2]

Dr. F. E. L. Priestley, in the magnificent introduction to the facsimile reprint of the third edition of *Political Justice,* traces the indebtedness of Henry George's *Progress and Poverty* to William Godwin. He reminds us that after the conservative reaction and repression of the 1820's, a new radical movement enrolled Douglas Jerrold, friend and protégé of Godwin, to serve the radical cause in the pages of *Punch.* James Watson issued a reprint of the third edition of *Political Justice* in 1798. Chartist periodicals quoted generously from it and from the *Enquirer.* In America, James Ogilvie, Orestes Brownson, William Ellery Channing, Bronson Alcott, and Charles Brockden Brown derived inspiration and specific instruction from Godwin's pages. William Thompson's work in the English school of socialism is "saturated with the spirit of Godwin" and transmits many Godwinian ideas to the followers of Robert Owen. Through Thompson and the Saint-Simonians, Godwin's theories of surplus value and of the final dwindling-away of the state pass on to Karl Marx. The British

Fabians of the end of the century have a strong Godwin flavor, and Oscar Wilde's *The Soul of Man under Socialism* raises seven of Godwin's issues: the accumulation of property is harmful to rich and poor alike; any form of collectivism is objectionable; marriage in its present form must disappear with the abolition of "private property"; every form of government is inimical to individualism; crime is error in judgment and punishment is always ineffectual; the machine should set man free from his grinding labor; and science will free man from disease and assure general longevity. H. G. Wells's *Men Like Gods* rehearses faithfully the Godwin doctrines of anarchism, the importance of sincerity, imperfect institutions as a necessary stage in the gradual abolition of government, marriage and the problem of population, and an almost religious faith in the sure triumph of truth.

In initial effect, widely eclectic derivation, and final influence, the *Enquiry concerning Political Justice* fully merits the modest praise of Godwin's friendly-enemy Sir James Mackintosh, in his essay in the *Edinburgh Review:* "He has . . . deserved the respect of all those, whatever may be their opinions, who still wish that some men in England may think for themselves, even at the risk of thinking wrong; but more especially of the friends of liberty, to whose cause he has courageously adhered." [3] Out of the many genres in which he wrote and the many conditions under which he published his work, a dominant impression of indomitable freshness and hopefulness emerges. When contrasted with the sentimentalism of Rousseau and the bleak mechanistic theory of utilitarianism, Godwin's work is all the more remarkable. When contrasted with the subsequent philosophies of Darwinism, with its integral connection with the animal world, and Freudianism, with its tyranny of the subconscious and the subrational, it does not in the least lose its bloom.

Any attempt to assess the importance and the continuing influence of the writings of William Godwin ought to start with his rare ability to relate diverse philosophical and political tendencies. This study has shown Godwin as the heir of Locke's epistemology, radical Protestantism, Roman republicanism, Rousseau's naturalism, and the political theories of Helvétius and d'Holbach. Godwin's remarkable achievement is not the diversity of the strands but the unity and uniqueness of the weaving. They all influenced Godwin profoundly, became part of the man himself, and were assimilated in a new, creative, and influential burst of literary energy.

It would be temptingly simple to consider the man and his works in the different eras of his life and in the varying genres of his writing. In a sense, this is what we have done. But such a segmentation ought not blind us to the primacy of the sectarian clergyman who came to London to inform men through the exercise of reason and to be the prophet of a secular Kingdom of God in which each man stands solitary, fulfilled, and sane. Just as segmentation must not obscure the centrality of the minister of rationality, so the many roles the man played and the many genres in which the author wrote must not, by sheer multiplicity, blind us to a central, extraordinary combination—the legal mind that produces an *Enquiry concerning Political Justice* replying to the leading jurists of England, and the ardent spirit which asserts Romantic individualism and produces the novel of sentiment. We will always be in Hazlitt's debt, therefore, for the satirical gimlet eye that saw Godwin's unique quality as his thoroughgoing habit of thought and action. Wherever his mind led him he followed; whatever logic built, he lived in securely and with no reference to all the popular shifts of public opinion.

His unusual concern for childhood and his unbounded faith in the educative process made him a modern man one hundred and fifty years ago. But his major lack is related to the very concern and faith that made him modern. He never seemed able to recognize the power of evil. He saw and exposed to the gaze of his contemporaries the operation of evil in government. He recognized this political evil as so pervasive and invincible that only the dissolution of government itself could end the evil. But he seemed quite unable to see evil as an integral and continuing part of the nature of man, not to be reasoned gently away, but lived with realistically to the end. Thus the same great passage which reflects Godwin's power of intellectual analysis along with his indomitable hopefulness for the future of mankind is also the measure of his weakness and of a constitutional myopia no experience could penetrate. This passage is found in the Epilogue to *Thoughts on Man, His Nature, Productions, and Discoveries,* published in 1831:

Let us then pay to human virtue the honour that is justly its due! Imagination is indeed a marvellous power; but imagination never equalled history, the achievements which man has actually performed. It is in vain that the man of contemplation sits down in his closet; it is in vain that the poet yields the reins to enthusiasm and fancy: there is something in the realities of life, that excites the mind infinitely more, than is in the power of the most exalted reverie. . . . Let then no man, in the supercilious spirit of a fancied disdain, allow himself to detract from our common nature. We are ourselves the models of all the excellence that the human mind can conceive. There have been men, whose virtues may well redeem all the contempt with which satire and detraction have sought to overwhelm our species. There have been memorable periods in the history of man, when the best, the most generous and exalted sentiments have swallowed up and obliterated all that was of an opposite character. And it is but just, that those by whom these things are fairly considered, should anticipate the progress of our nature, and believe that human understanding and human virtue will hereafter accomplish such things as the heart of man has never yet been daring enough to conceive.[4]

Notes and References

Chapter One

1. Russell Noyes, *English Romantic Poetry and Prose* (New York, 1956), p. 375.
2. Charles Kegan Paul, *William Godwin: His Friends and Contemporaries* (London, 1879), I, 19.
3. *Ibid.*, I, 17.
4. *Ibid.*, I, 9.
5. James A. Preu, *The Dean and the Anarchist* (Tallahassee, 1959), p. 15 f.
6. *The Spirit of the Age: or Contemporary Portraits* (1825), in *The Complete Works of William Hazlitt*, ed. P. P. Howe (London, 1932), XI, 16 f.
7. B. Sprague Allen, "The Reaction Against William Godwin," *Modern Philology*, XVI, No. 5 (September, 1918), 57.

Chapter Two

1. Noyes, "Introduction," p. xxviii.
2. *The Dean and the Anarchist*, p. 15.
3. Paul, I, 14.
4. J. Middleton Murry, *Heaven—and Earth* (London, 1938), p. 262.
5. *The Marriage of Heaven and Hell*, "Proverbs of Hell."
6. Murry, p. 259.
7. "Platonism in William Godwin's *Political Justice*," *Modern Language Quarterly*, IV (March, 1934), 63.
8. Leslie Stephen, "William Godwin's Novels," *National Review*, XXXVIII (February, 1902), 911.
9. B. Sprague Allen, "William Godwin as a Sentimentalist," *PMLA*, XXXIII (Baltimore, 1918), 7.
10. Charles Cestre, *John Thelwall, a Pioneer of Democracy and Social Reform in England during the French Revolution* (London, 1906), Appendix.

11. Hazlitt, XI, 27.

12. Paul, I, 312.

13. "The Reaction Against William Godwin," 71.

14. Murry, p. 257.

15. *The Dean and the Anarchist*, p. 15 f.

16. Murry, p. 260.

17. D. H. Monro, *Godwin's Moral Philosophy, an Interpretation of William Godwin* (London, 1953), p. 7.

18. B. Sprague Allen, "William Godwin's Influence upon John Thelwall," *PMLA*, XXXVII (Menasha, Wisc., 1922), 677.

19. "William Godwin's Novels," 911.

20. William Godwin, *Thoughts on Man, His Nature, Productions and Discoveries* (London, 1831), "Preface."

21. Hazlitt, XI, 18.

22. "William Godwin's Novels," 908.

23. Murry, p. 261.

24. Paul, I, 10.

25. Murry, p. 256.

26. Monro, p. 6.

27. Hazlitt, XI, 19.

28. David Fleisher, *William Godwin, a Study in Liberalism* (London, 1951), p. 62.

29. Monro, p. 6.

30. Hazlitt, XI, 27.

31. Francesco Cardasco, *William Godwin, a Handlist of Critical Notices and Studies* (Brooklyn, 1950).

32. James Arthur Preu, *Antimonarchism in Swift and Godwin* (Tallahassee, 1955), p. 11.

33. *Ibid.*, p. 17.

34. Jonathan Swift, *Gulliver's Travels*, in *The Portable Swift* (New York, 1948), p. 424.

35. *Ibid.*, pp. 234-35.

36. *Antimonarchism in Swift and Godwin*, p. 18.

37. Swift, pp. 469-70.

38. *Ibid.*, p. 481.

39. *Ibid.*, p. 418.

40. *Antimonarchism in Swift and Godwin*, p. 14.

41. Paul, I, 12.

42. William Blake, "Preface" from *Milton*, in Noyes, p. 224.

43. Paul, I, 59.

44. *The Dean and the Anarchist*, p. 15 f.

45. Paul, I, 68.

46. William Wordsworth, *The Prelude*, Bk. II, lines 108-9.

47. Robert Southey, "Letter to Caroline Bowles, Feb. 13, 1824," *The Correspondence of Robert Southey with Caroline Bowles* (London, 1881), p. 52.

48. Wordsworth, Bk. XI, lines 109-18.

49. Murry, p. 257.

50. Hazlitt, XI, 16.

51. Henry Crabb Robinson, *Diary, Reminiscences, and Correspondence,* 2nd ed. (London, 1869), I, 31.

52. "William Godwin's Novels," 912.

53. "The Reaction Against William Godwin," 57.

54. *Diary, Reminiscences, and Correspondence,* 3rd ed. (London and New York, 1872), I, 21.

55. Monro, p. 4.

56. Percy Bysshe Shelley, *The Letters of Percy Bysshe Shelley* (London, 1914), II, 211.

57. Hazlitt, XI, 16.

Chapter Three

1. Paul, I, 117.

2. "To William Godwin," first published in the *Morning Chronicle,* January 10, 1795. The last six lines were sent in a letter to Southey, dated December 17, 1794.

3. "William Godwin's Novels," 911.

4. Fleisher, p. 38; also Paul, I, 358.

5. "The Reaction Against William Godwin," 57.

6. Paul, I, 16.

7. *Ibid.,* 26.

8. *Ibid.,* 357.

9. *Ibid.,* 28.

10. *Ibid.,* 29.

11. *Cursory Strictures* (London, 1794), p. 10.

12. *Ibid.,* p. 11.

13. *Ibid.,* p. 17.

14. *Ibid.,* p. 25.

15. *Memoirs of William Godwin,* pamphlet, New York Public Library, Ford Collection.

16. Hazlitt, XI, 26.

17. *Ibid.,* 17.

18. *Considerations on Lord Grenville's and Mr. Pitt's Bills* (London, 1795), p. 2.

19. *Ibid.,* p. 17.

20. Fleisher, p. 29.

21. *Considerations,* p. 23.

22. *Ibid.*, p. 27.
23. *Ibid.*, p. 31.
24. *Ibid.*, p. 85.
25. Paul, I, 292.
26. *Thoughts Occasioned by the Perusal of Dr. Parr's Spital Sermon* (London, 1801).
27. *Ibid.*, p. 22.
28. *Considerations*, p. 81.
29. *Thoughts Occasioned by the Perusal of Dr. Parr's Spital Sermon*, pp. 10-12.
30. *Ibid.*, pp. 10-12.
31. *Ibid.*, pp. 80-82.
32. *A Topographical Description of the Western Territory of North America* (London, 1792).
33. Paul, I, 215.
34. *Ibid.*, p. 232.
35. *Ibid.*, p. 272.
36. *Ibid.*, p. 273.
37. Monro, p. 3.
38. "Reaction Against William Godwin," 61.
39. *Ibid.*, 60.
40. "William Godwin's Novels," 915.
41. Paul, II, 321.
42. *Ibid.*, II, 359.
43. "William Godwin's Novels," 908.
44. Paul, I, 68.
45. Murry, p. 263.
46. Hazlitt, XI, 27; also Murry, p. 260.
47. Paul, II, 106.
48. B. Sprague Allen, "William Godwin and the Stage," *PMLA,* New Series XXVIII (Baltimore, 1920), 365.
49. Paul, I, 40.
50. *Ibid.*, I, 78.
51. *Ibid.*, II, 157.
52. Cestre, p. 29.
53. "William Godwin's Influence upon John Thelwall," 676.
54. "The Reaction Against William Godwin," 62.
55. Paul, I, 117.
56. Godwin's *Journal*, Copy no. 21 (London: Charles Mitchell Ltd.), New York Public Library Rare Book Room; "Tragical Consequences or a Disaster at Deal," being an unpublished letter of William Godwin, dated Wednesday, November 18, 1789. (London: Fytton Armstrong, 1931), New York Public Library Rare Book Room.

57. Paul, I, 312.

58. *Ibid.*, II, 261.

59. *Ibid.*, I, 330.

60. *Ibid.*, II, 323.

61. "The Reaction Against William Godwin," 75.

62. William Kingsland, "Shelley and Godwin," *Poet-Lore,* X (Boston, 1898), 390.

63. *Ibid.*, X, 390.

64. *Ibid.*, X, 390.

65. Paul, II, 214-16.

66. *The Elopement of Percy Bysshe Shelley and Mary Wollstonecraft Godwin,* as narrated by William Godwin (Bibliophile Society copyright 1911), p. 11.

67. Kingsland, X, 394.

68. *Ibid.*, X, 394.

69. Paul, II, 231.

70. Murry, p. 265.

71. Fleisher, p. 53.

72. Kingsland, X, 396.

73. Paul, II, 277.

74. *Ibid.*, II, 302, 304.

75. *Enquirer* (London, 1797), p. 87.

76. *Ibid.*, p. 370.

77. *Essay on Sepulchres,* "Preface" (London, 1809; New York, 1809), p. vi.

78. *Ibid.*, p. ix.

79. *Ibid.*, p. i.

80. *Ibid.*, p. 6.

81. *Ibid.*, p. 10.

82. Paul, II, 321.

83. *Of Population, an Enquiry concerning the Power of Increase in the Numbers of Mankind, Being an Answer to Mr. Malthus's Essay on that Subject* (London, 1820), p. iv.

84. Fleisher, p. 52.

85. *Thoughts on Man,* p. v.

86. *Ibid.*, p. 470.

87. *The Genius of Christianity Unveiled,* Editor's Preface.

88. *Ibid.*

Chapter Four

1. *The Adventures of Caleb Williams or Things as They Are* (New York, 1960). Preface prepared for the 1794 edition but withdrawn

for fear "the humble novelist might be shown to be constructively a traitor." October 29, 1795, p. xxiv.

2. Paul, I, 20.

3. "Godwin's Own Account of *Caleb Williams,* as written for insertion in the edition of *Fleetwood* when that novel was reprinted in Bentley's 'Standard Novels' as No. XXII (1832)," in the Rinehart Edition named in footnote 1, pp. xxix-xxx.

4. "William Godwin and the Stage," note, 374.

5. *Memoirs of William Godwin,* p. 15.

6. *Ibid.,* p. 16.

7. *Ibid.,* "Preface."

8. *Caleb Williams,* p. 376.

9. *Ibid.,* pp. 377-78.

10. *Ibid.,* p. 159.

11. Monro, p. 91.

12. *Ibid.,* p. 88.

13. "William Godwin as a Sentimentalist," 9.

14. *Memoirs,* p. 16.

15. *Caleb Williams,* p. xxx.

16. *St. Leon: a Tale of the Sixteenth Century* (London, 1850), "Advertisement."

17. *Biographia Literaria,* Chap. xiv.

18. *St. Leon,* "Preface."

19. *Ibid.,* p. 93.

20. *Ibid.,* p. 478.

21. *Ibid.,* p. 85.

22. *Ibid.,* p. 248.

23. *Ibid.,* p. 400.

24. *Ibid.,* p. 82.

25. *Ibid.,* p. 282.

26. *Ibid.,* p. 210.

27. *Ibid.,* p. 361, or "William Godwin as a Sentimentalist," 18.

28. *Ibid.,* p. 433.

29. "William Godwin as a Sentimentalist," 18.

30. "William Godwin and the Stage," note, 362.

31. *Ibid.,* 538.

32. *Fleetwood: or the New Man of Feeling* (New York, 1805), "Preface."

33. *Ibid.,* p. vi.

34. *Ibid.,* p. ix.

35. *Fleetwood,* II, 47.

36. "William Godwin as a Sentimentalist," 23.

37. *Ibid.,* 26; also Kegan Paul, *William Godwin,* I, 42.
38. "William Godwin as a Sentimentalist," 28; or *Fleetwood,* II, 31.
39. *Fleetwood,* I, 161.
40. *Ibid.,* 166.
41. *Ibid.,* 13.
42. *Ibid.,* 238.
43. Hazlitt, XI, 25.
44. *Memoirs,* p. 18.
45. *Fleetwood,* I, 238.
46. Fred Lewis Pattee, "Introduction," *Wieland, or the Trans-formation* (New York, 1926), p. xvii.
47. *Mandeville* (Edinburgh, 1817), I, 190 ff.
48. "William Godwin and the Stage," 370.
49. Adeline E. Glasheen, "Shelley's First Published Review of *Mandeville," Modern Language Notes,* LIX (March, 1924), 172.
50. "William Godwin as a Sentimentalist," 12.
51. *Cloudesley* (London, 1830), I, 231.
52. *Mandeville,* III, 124.
53. *Vindication of the Rights of Women* (London, 1798), p. 150.
54. *Cloudesley,* III, 341.
55. "William Godwin as a Sentimentalist," 11.
56. "A *Review of Cloudesley: a Tale,* by the Author of *Caleb Wil-liams," Edinburgh Review,* LI (April, 1830), 146.
57. *Ibid.,* 150.
58. *Ibid.,* 151.
59. *Ibid.,* 155.
60. *Ibid.,* 154.
61. *Ibid.,* 157.
62. *Deloraine* (London, 1833), "Preface."
63. Pattee, p. xvii.
64. "The Reaction Against William Godwin," 65.
65. Monro, p. 57.
66. "The Reaction Against William Godwin," 63.
67. Boston, 1802, p. 14.
68. *Ibid.,* p. 19.
69. *Ibid.,* pp. 15-17.
70. *Ibid.,* pp. 17-19.
71. *Thoughts Occasioned by Dr. Parr's Spital Sermon,* I, 24.
72. Paul, I, 14.
73. "William Godwin and the Stage," 358.
74. Paul, II, 77.
75. *The Iron Chest,* p. 5.

Chapter Five

1. Murry, p. 254.
2. Paul, I, 5.
3. *Ibid.,* 6.
4. *Ibid.,* 7.
5. *Ibid.,* 9.
6. *Ibid.,* 11.
7. *Ibid.,* 12.
8. Murry, p. 254.
9. Paul, II, 129.
10. Murry, p. 266.
11. *The History of England, for the Use of Schools and Young Persons* (London, 1815), "Preface."
12. Fleischer, p. 16.
13. Murry, p. 266
14. Paul, II, 118.
15. *Fables,* "Preface," p. 5.
16. Paul, II, 133.
17. *Ibid.,* I, 12.
18. *Ibid.,* 79.
19. Hazlitt, XI, 26.
20. *Ibid.,* 26.
21. *Life of Geoffrey Chaucer* (London, 1803), "Preface," p. i.
22. *Ibid.,* p. iv.
23. *Ibid.,* p. 478.
24. *Ibid.,* p. 483.
25. *Ibid.,* p. 71.
26. *Ibid.,* pp. 360-61.
27. *Ibid.,* p. 399.
28. "Preface," pp. ix, x.
29. *Lives of Edward and John Philips* (London, 1809, 1815), "Preface," p. vi.
30. *Ibid.,* p. 8.
31. *Ibid.,* p. 266.
32. *Ibid.,* p. 126.
33. *Ibid.,* p. 157.
34. *Ibid.,* p. 313.
35. *Ibid.,* p. 208.
36. *Ibid.,* p. 68.
37. *Ibid.,* p. 159.
38. Hazlitt, XI, 28.
39. Murry, p. 255.

40. Fleisher, p. 56.
41. *Lives of Necromancers* (London, 1834; New York, 1838, 1847, 1876), "Preface," p. xxix.
42. *Ibid.*, p. vii.
43. *Ibid.*, p. ix.
44. *Ibid.*, p. xii.
45. *Ibid.*, p. 465.

Chapter Six

1. Somervell, p. 32.
2. Noyes, p. 177.
3. Sir James Mackintosh, *Edinburgh Review*, XXV (1815), 485.
4. *Thoughts on Man*, p. 470.

Selected Bibliography

PRIMARY SOURCES

Since Godwin's works are listed by dates in the Chronology, and by genre in the context, they are here arranged alphabetically.

An Account of the Seminary that will be opened on Monday the Fourth Day of August at Epsom in Surrey. London: n.p., 1783 (anon.).

The Adventures of Caleb Williams, or Things as They Are. 3 vols. London: B. Crosby, 1794; 1796; 1831; rptd., 1903; tr. French, 1797. Edition used for footnotes: New York: Rinehart & Co., Inc., 1960.

Antonio: a Tragedy in Five Acts. London: n.p., 1800; New York: D. Longworth, at the Dramatic Repository, Shakespeare Gallery, 1806.

Cloudesley: a Tale. 3 vols. London: Henry Colburn and Richard Bentley, 1830.

Considerations on Lord Grenville's and Mr. Pitt's Bills Concerning Treasonable and Seditious Practices, and Unlawful Assemblies. By a "Lover of Order." London: J. Johnson, 1795.

Cursory Strictures on the Charge Delivered by Lord Chief Justice Eyre to the Grand Jury, October 2, 1794. First published in *The Morning Chronicle,* October 21, 1794. London: D. I. Eaton, 1794 (anon.).

Damon and Delia. London: n.p., 1783.

Deloraine. 3 vols. London: R. Bentley, 1833.

The Elopement of Percy Bysshe Shelley and Mary Wollstonecraft Godwin. Privately printed, 1911, by the Bibliophile Society.

The Enquirer. Reflections on Education, Manners, and Literature. In a Series of Essays. London: B. B. and J. Robinson, 1797; 1823.

An Enquiry concerning the Principles of Political Justice, and its Influence on General Virtue and Happiness. 2 vols. London, Dublin: B. B. and J. Robinson, 1793; London, Philadelphia, 1796; London, 1798; ed. H. S. Salt, 1890; ed. R. A. Preston, 1926 (abridged).

Edition used for footnotes: *Enquiry concerning Political Justice and its Influence on Morals and Happiness,* Photographic Facsimile of the Third Edition Corrected, Edited, with Variant Readings of the First and Second Editions and with a Critical Introduction and Notes, by F. E. L. Priestley. 3 vols. The University of Toronto Press, 1946.

Essay on Sepulchres: of a Proposal for erecting Some Memorial of the Illustrious Dead in All Ages on the Spot Where Their Remains have been Interred. London: W. Miller, 1809; New York: M. and W. Ward, 1809.

Essays never before Published. Ed. C. K. Paul. London: Henry S. King & Co., 1873.

Fables, Ancient and Modern. By Edward Baldwin, Esq. (pseud.) 2 vols. London: Hodgkins, 1805.

Faulkener: a Tragedy. London: Richard Phillips, 1807.

Fleetwood: or, The New Man of Feeling. 3 vols. London: S. Gould and Co., 1805; 2 vols. New York: I. Riley & Co., 1805; 3 vols. Paris: n.p., 1805; London: Bentley's Standard Novels, 1832.

The Herald of Literature. London: n.p., 1784. British Museum (anon.).

History of the Commonwealth of England, from its Commencement to the Restoration of Charles the Second. 4 vols. London: n.p., 1824-1828.

The History of England, for the Use of Schools and Young Persons. By Edward (also Edwin) Baldwin, Esq. (pseud.). London: Juvenile Library, 1815.

The History of Greece. By Edward Baldwin, Esq. (pseud.). London: Juvenile Library, 1811.

The History of the Life of William Pitt, Earl of Chatham. London: n.p., 1783 (anon.).

The History of Rome. By Edward Baldwin, Esq. (pseud.). London: Juvenile Library, 1809.

Imogen, a Pastoral Romance. London: n.p., 1784.

Italian Letters. London: n.p., 1783.

The Life of Geoffrey Chaucer, the Early English Poet: including Memoirs of His Near Friend and Kinsman, John of Gaunt, Duke of Lancaster: with Sketches of the Manners, Opinions, Arts and Literature of England in the Fourteenth Century. 2 vols. London: Richard Phillips, 1803; 4 vols. London: Richard Phillips, 1804; tr. German, 1812.

The Life of Lady Jane Grey, and of Guildford Dudley, her Husband. By Theophilus Marcliffe (pseud.). London: Hodgkins, 1806.

The Lives of Edward and John Philips, Nephews and Pupils of Milton.

London: Longman, Hurst, Rees, Orme, and Brown, 1809; London: Longman, Hurst, Rees, Orme, and Brown, 1815.

The Lives of the Necromancers: or, an Account of the Most Eminent Persons in Successive Ages, Who have Claimed for Themselves, or to Whom has been Imputed by Others, the Exercise of Magical Power. London: Frederick J. Mason, 1834; New York, 1835, 1847, 1876.

The Looking Glass: a True History of the Early Years of an Artist. By Theophilus Marcliffe (pseud.). London: Hodgkins, 1805; rptd. facs. 1885.

Mandeville: a Tale of the Seventeenth Century in England. 3 vols. Edinburgh: n.p., 1817; 2 vols. New York: n.p., 1818; tr. French, 1819.

Memoirs of the Author of a Vindication of the Rights of Women. London: n.p., 1798; Philadelphia (*The Memoirs of Mary Wollstonecraft Godwin*): Printed by James Carey, 1799; ed. W. C. Durrant, 1927; ed. J. M. Murry, 1928.

A New Guide to the English Tongue. By Edward Baldwin, Esq. (pseud.) and M. J. Godwin. London: Juvenile Library, 1809.

Outlines of English Grammar; partly abridged from Mr. Hazlitt's New and Improved Grammar. By Edward Baldwin, Esq. (pseud.). London: Juvenile Library, 1810.

The Pantheon, or Ancient History of the Gods of Greece and Rome. By Edward Baldwin, Esq. (pseud.). London: Hodgkins, 1806.

Of Population: an Enquiry concerning the Power of Increase in the Numbers of Mankind; being an Answer to Mr. Malthus's Essay. London: Longman, Hurst, Rees, Orme, and Brown, 1820; Paris, 1821.

A Reply to an Answer to Cursory Strictures, Supposed to be Wrote by Judge [Sir Frances] Buller, by the Author of Cursory Strictures. London: D. I. Eaton, 1794.

Sketches of History, in Six Sermons. London: n.p., 1784.

St. Leon: a Tale of the Sixteenth Century. 3 vols. London: Richard Bentley, 1799; 4 vols. 1800; 2 vols. Dublin: n.p., 1800; 2 vols. Alexandria, Va., 1801; London: Bentley's Standard Novels, 1831; in *The Novelist*, Vol. II, 1840; tr. French, 1799.

Thoughts Occasioned by Dr. Parr's Spital Sermon. London: n.p., 1801.

Thoughts on Man, his Nature, Productions and Discourses. London: n.p., 1831.

Tragical Consequences, or a Disaster at Deal, being an unpublished letter dated Wed. Nov. 18, 1789, and remarks thereon by Edmund Blunden.

SECONDARY SOURCES

1. *Books*

BRAILSFORD, H. N. *Shelley, Godwin and Their Circle.* London: William
& Norgate, 1913. Vigorous analysis of the intellectual and political
climate in which Shelley and Godwin lived.

BROWN, FORD K. *The Life of William Godwin.* London: J. M. Dent
and Sons, Ltd., 1926. Basic study of Godwin, but chiefly biographical rather than intellectual or literary. Excellent bibliography of primary materials.

BULLER, SIR FRANCIS. *Answer to Cursory Strictures on a Charge Delivered to the Grand Jury, October 2, 1794.* London: Daniel Isaac
Eaton, 1794. Legal debate; published as a pamphlet.

*The Charge Delivered by The Right Honourable Sir James Eyre, Lord
Chief Justice of His Majesty's Court of Common Plea and One
of the Commissioners Named in a Special Commission of Oyer
and Terminer, issued under the Great Seal of Great Britain, To
enquire of Certain High Treasons and Misprisons of Treason,
Within the County of Middlesex, To the Grand Jury, At the
Session House on Clerkenwell Green, on Thursday the 2d Day
of October, 1794.* Published at the request of the Grand Jury; by
Daniel Isaac Eaton, 1794. Legal document essential to understanding of Godwin's reply.

CORDASCO, FRANCESCO. *William Godwin, a Handlist of Critical Notices
and Studies, Eighteenth Century Bibligraphical Pamphlet No. 9.*
Ed. Tristram Walker Metcalfe. Brooklyn: Long Island University
Press, 1950. Helpful, but brief.

Criticism of the Novels of Godwin. Anonymous pamphlet, New York
Public Library, Ford Collection, A.G.H. p.v. 13, no. 5. Too keen
a sense of the "Rights of Women" in Godwin's female characters.

DOWDEN, EDWARD. "Theorists of Revolution: Godwin, Mary Wollstone-
craft," in *The French Revolution and English Literature.* London:
K. Paul, Trench, Trubner & Co., Ltd., 1897 (Princeton Lectures).
Good for political theory; no discussion of novels or plays.

DUBOIS, EDWARD. *St. Godwin; a Tale of the Sixteenth, Seventeenth
and Eighteenth Centuries.* By Count Reginald de St. Leon
(pseud.). London: J. Wright, 1800. Obvious and scurrilous
parody of Godwin's *St. Leon.*

FLEISHER, DAVID. *William Godwin, a Study in Liberalism.* London:
G. Allen & Unwin, Ltd., 1951. Best study to date of Godwin's
ideas and themes. Stronger in philosophy than literary criticism.

GRYLLS, ROSALIE GLYNN. *William Godwin and His World.* London:

Bibliography

Odhams Press, 1953. Godwin placed in the social and political milieu of the Late Enlightenment.

HAMILTON, ELIZABETH. *Memoirs of Modern Philosophers.* London: G. G. & J. Robinson, 1800. Fictitious, highly imaginative and pejorative judgment of the Liberal philosophers.

HAZLITT, WILLIAM. *The Spirit of the Age: or Contemporary Portraits,* in *The Complete Works of William Hazlitt.* Ed. P. P. Howe, 21 vols. London: J. M. Dent and Sons, 1932. Richly rhetorical and picturesque views of Godwin through the eyes of a satirical contemporary.

LUCAS, CHARLES. *The Infernal Quixote.* 4 vols. London: n.p., 1801. Fictitious and libelous characterization of the Godwinian thinker.

MALTHUS, THOMAS ROBERT. *An Essay on the Principle of Population as It Affects the Future Improvement of Society. With Remarks on the Speculations of Mr. Godwin, M. Condorcet, and Other Writers.* London: J. Johnson, 1798. Major philosophic debate on problem of population and subsistence.

Memoirs of William Godwin. Anonymous pamphlet, New York Public Library, Ford Collection, A.G.H. p.v. 13, no. 5. Good but limited contemporaneous memoir.

MONRO, D. H. *Godwin's Moral Philosophy, an Interpretation of William Godwin.* London: Oxford University Press, 1953. Trenchant presentation of Godwin as moral philosopher in essay, tract, and novel.

MURRY, JOHN MIDDLETON. *Heaven—and Earth.* London: J. Cape, 1938. (Same as Chapter VIII in *Heroes of Thought.* New York: J. Messner, 1938.) Eloquent but one-sided statement of Godwin's indebtedness to his Protestant inheritance.

PARR, SAMUEL. "A Spital Sermon, Preached at Christ Church, upon Easter Tuesday, April 15, 1800; to which are added Notes," in *Works,* Ed. Johnstone. London: Longman, Rees, Orme, Brown, & Green, 1828, II, 387. Treatment of Godwin and Godwinism as major threats to public morality.

PAUL, CHARLES KEGAN. *William Godwin: His Friends and Contemporaries.* 2 vols. London: Henry S. King & Co., 1876. Basic source of Godwin's diaries, letters, and autobiographical fragments.

PREU, JAMES ARTHUR. *Antimonarchism in Swift and Godwin.* Florida State University Studies, no. 19. Tallahassee: F.S.U., 1955. Thorough documentation of Godwin's debt to Swift's *Gulliver's Travels.*

———. *The Dean and the Anarchist.* Florida State University Studies, no. 33. Tallahassee: F.S.U., 1959. Excellent references to early diaries and to the political climate leading up to publication of *Political Justice*.

PROBY, WILLIAM C. *Modern Philosophy and Barbarism: or, a Comparison between the Theory of Godwin and the Practice of Lycurgus*. London: R. H. Westley, 1798. Godwin as proponent of a revised Spartanism.

ROBINSON, HENRY CRABB. *Diary, Reminiscences, and Correspondence*. 2 vols. ed. Thomas Sadler, 2nd ed. London: Macmillan & Co., 1869. Important to illustrate both Godwin's early fame and later disfavor.

ROBINSON, VICTOR. *William Godwin and Mary Wollstonecraft*. Pamphlet in series *Lives of Great Altrurians*. New York: The Altrurians, 1907. Good biographical material on Mary Wollstonecraft.

SHELLEY, PERCY BYSSHE. *The Letters of Percy Bysshe Shelley*. 2 vols. ed. Ingpen. London: G. Bell & Sons, Ltd., 1914. The adulation of a disciple and the disillusionment of a son-in-law.

WOODCOCK, GEORGE. *William Godwin: a Biographical Study with a foreword by Herbert Read*. London: The Porcupine Press, 1946. Balanced treatment of both life and ideas.

2. Periodicals

ALLEN, B. SPRAGUE. "The Reaction Against William Godwin," *Modern Philology*, XVI, no. 5 (Sept. 1918), 57-75. Godwin's own frank assessment of his fall from public esteem. Excellent treatment of anti-Godwinian novels.

——. "William Godwin and the Stage," *PMLA*, Baltimore, 1920. New Series XXVIII, 358-74. Valuable treatment of themes common to the novels and the plays.

——. "William Godwin as a Sentimentalist," *PMLA*, Baltimore, 1918. XXXIII, no. 1, 1-29. Strong case for Godwin's profound influence as arising from paradoxical union of reason and feeling.

——. "William Godwin's Influence upon John Thelwall," *PMLA*, Menasha, Wisc., 1922, XXXVII, 662-82. The embarrassment to Godwin of his young, over-zealous disciples.

DEEN, FLOYD HARRISON. "The Genesis of Martin Faber in *Caleb Williams*," *Modern Language Notes*, LIX (May 1944), 315-17. Detailed analysis of literary similarities. Both indebtedness and originality are established.

GLASHEEN, ADALINE E. "Shelley's First Published Review of *Mandeville*," *Modern Language Notes*, LIX (March 1944), 172-73. Documentary evidence for Godwin's indiscreet use of a personal letter for publicity.

Bibliography

HAZLITT, WILLIAM. "Mr. Godwin," *Edinburgh Review,* April 1830. Later incorporated in *Contemporary Portraits.*

KINGSLAND, WILLIAM G. "Shelley and Godwin," *Poet-Lore,* (Boston, 1898) X, 389-97. Judicious selections from the Shelley-Godwin correspondence.

PREU, JAMES. "Swift's Influence on Godwin's Doctrine of Anarchism," *Journal of the History of Ideas,* XV (1954), 371-83. Essentially similar to thesis of *The Dean and the Anarchist.*

PRIESTLEY, F. E. L. "Platonism in William Godwin's *Political Justice,*" *Modern Language Quarterly,* IV (March 1943), 63-69. Godwin's political tract viewed as Eighteenth-Century Platonism rather than the tradition of Locke, Helvétius, and Hartley.

"A Review of *Cloudesley: a Tale,* by the Author of *Caleb Williams,*" Art. VI. *Edinburgh Review,* LI (April 1830), 144-59. The popular romance maimed by a metaphysician who makes all his characters extremes of vice or virtue.

ROBERTS, CHARLES W. "The Influence of Godwin on Wordsworth's Letter to the Bishop of Llandaff (Richard Watson)," *Studies in Philology,* N.C.U. Phil. Club, XXIX (Baltimore, 1932), 588-606. A fair case for Godwinian influence on Wordsworth.

STEPHEN, SIR LESLIE. "William Godwin's Novels," *National Review,* XXXVIII (February 1902), 908-23; also in *Studies of a Biographer,* vol. 3. London: Duckworth & Co., 1898-1902, and New York: G. P. Putnam's Sons, 1902. A thoroughly negative study; Godwin as "the superlative bore."

STONE, E. "*Caleb Williams* and *Martin Faber:* a Contrast," *Modern Language Notes,* LXIII (Nov. 1947), 480-83. Argument against the usual asumption that Simm's novel was derived from Godwin's original.

Index

(The Data Processing Division of the University of South Florida kindly assisted in the preparation of this index.)

Aaron (Biblical), 56
Abbas, King of Persia, 115
Account of the Seminary for the Instruction of Twelve Pupils, An, 21, 127
Acts of the Apostles, 42
Addison, Joseph, 76
Adulation, 62
Adventures of Mademoiselle St. Phale, The (anonymous), 85
Agar, Thomas, 135
Akers, Robert, 123
Alcott, Bronson, 145
Aliens Act, The, 51
Anarchism, 42, 55, 146
Ancient History (Rollin), 47
Anti-Godwinian novels, 112-14
Anti-Jacobin, 64, 69
Antonio, A Tragedy in Five Acts, 114-16
Arnold, Matthew, 19
Arnot, John, 67, 71
Associationalism, 43
Atheism, 19, 53, 55, 57, 108
Aubrey, John, 135
Augustine, St., 20

Bacon, Sir Francis, 136
Bailie, James Kennedy, 103
Baldwin, Edward, 124, 127, 129
Ballantyne, James, 67, 71

Beaupuy, Captain Michel, 120
Bell, Dr. James, 67, 71
Benefactors, 122
Benevolence, 28-29, 36, 39-40, 50, 73, 81, 87-89, 94, 101, 104
Berkeley, George, Bishop, 78
Bernardin, 92
Bible, The Holy, 20, 42-43, 56, 82, 103, 113
Biographer, 84, 130
Biographia Literaria (Coleridge), 91
Blake, William, 19, 23, 32
Blood, Fanny, 63
Bluebeard, 86
Bolingbroke, Henry, 131
Borderers, The (Wordsworth), 70, 120
Brown, Charles Brockden, 103, 112, 145
Browne, Sir Thomas, 78, 112
Brownson, Orestes, 145
Bunyan, John, 122
Burdett, Sir Francis, 69
Burke, Edmund, 21, 36, 51, 53, 60, 142
Burks, John Daly, 96
Butler, Samuel, 78
Byron, Anne Isabella, Lady, 86
Byron, George Gordon, Lord, 65, 74, 86, 94, 96, 99

Caesar, Julius, 114
Caleb Williams, 22, 76, 84-91, 96, 99, 103, 105-6, 108-9, 112-13, 115-16, 119, 126, 134
Calvinism, 19-20, 42, 56, 123

Calvin, John, 42, 134
Camillus, Marcus Furius, 108
Campbel, Dr. John, 91
Carlyle, Thomas, 19, 141
Channing, William Ellery, 145
Charlemagne, 108
Charles II, 142
Chateaubriand, François René, Vicomte de, 99
Chaucer, Geoffrey, 132-33
Childhood, 147
Children's books, 8, 55, 66, 74, 77, 100, 123-24, 129
Chivalry, 107, 116, 126, 134
Christianity, 20, 43
Clairmont, Jane "Claire," 65-66, 72, 74
Clairmont, Mrs. Mary Jane, 65
Clarges, Sir Thomas, 137
Classics, 130
Clergyman, 133, 147
Cloudesley: a Tale, 105-6, 109, 126, 134
Cohausen, Johann Heinrich, 91
Co-operation, 37
Coke, Sir Edward, 136
Cole, William, 125
Coleridge, Samuel Taylor, 19, 54-55, 57, 69-70
"Collections for the Life of Milton" (Aubrey), 135
Colman, George, 114, 118
Communism, 42, 145
Condillac, Étienne Bonnot, Abbé de, 43
Condorcet, Antoine Marie, Marquis de, 77
Congreve, William, 90
Considerations on Lord Grenville's and Mr. Pitt's Bills (Pamphlet), 60, 62
Contemporary Portraits (Hazlitt), 84
Cooke, William, 67, 71
Cooper, Thomas, 67-68, 119
Crime, 31, 33-34, 40, 76, 87-90, 105, 107, 109, 111, 118, 143, 146
Cromwell, Oliver, 50, 141-42

Cyphon, Theodore, 113

D'Holbach, Paul Henri Dietrich, Baron, 20, 44, 57, 146
Damon and Delia, Italian Letters, 85
Darwin, Charles, 77, 146
Daughter, 73
De L'Esprit (Helvétius), 20
De Quincey, Thomas, 121
Defoe, Daniel, 117
Deism, 19-20, 57
Deloraine, 105, 109-11, 126, 134
Democracy, 25, 30, 51
Determinism, 34
Dickens, Charles, 19, 100
Discourse on the Love of Our Country, A (Price), 48
Doctrine and Discipline of Divorce, The (Milton), 136
Drama, 84
Drayton, Michael, 137
Dryden, John, 78
Dunlap, William, 103, 112
Dyson, George, 67, 71

Ecclesiastical Polity (Hooker), 78
Edinburgh Review, The, 108, 146
Education, 125-26, 135, 138, 147
Edward III, 113, 131
Edwards, Jonathan, 42
Encyclopedists, French, 42, 44
English Review, The, 85
Enlightenment, The, 20
Enquirer: Reflections on Education, Manners and Literature, The, 44, 61, 76-77, 81, 145
Enquiry Concerning Political Justice, 21-23, 26-27, 41, 43-45, 51-52, 55, 58, 60, 62, 65, 70-72, 76-77, 79, 84-86, 89, 91, 98, 101, 103-4, 108-109, 112-14, 116, 129, 134, 142, 145-47
Epistemology, 43-44, 146
Essay on Population (Malthus), 52, 76-77, 79
Essay on Sepulchres, An, 78
Essayist, 22, 52, 55, 76-79, 82
Essays Never Before Published, 82

Index

Essays of Elia (Lamb), 70
Eugene Aram, A Tale (Bulwer-Lytton), 76
Evans, Richard, 19
Examiner, The, 105
Excursion, The (Wordsworth), 69
Eyre, Lord Chief Justice, 58

Fabians, 146
Fables, 128
Fables, Ancient and Modern, 127
Faraday, Michael, 42
Father, Godwin as, 66, 73, 75, 94, 97, 107, 119, 121-22, 126
Faulkener, A Tragedy in Prose, 114, 116-18
Fénelon, Archbishop of Cambray, 26, 39, 113
Fenwick, John, 70
Feudalism, 133-34
Fielding, Henry, 35, 38
Fleetwood, or The New Man of Feeling, 96-103, 105, 109, 116, 126
Fletcher, John, 137
Fox, Charles James, 35, 48
Frankenstein (Mary Shelley), 86, 121
Free will, 29, 44
Freedom, 31
French Revolution, The, 35, 47, 51, 53, 62, 121
Freudianism, 146
Friend, Godwin as, 55, 66, 71, 95, 99, 101, 110-11, 115, 117
Friends of William Godwin, 61, 65-66, 69-71, 74-76, 81, 130
"Friends of the People," 36

Gay, John, 43
Genius of Christianity Unveiled, The, 82
George, Henry, 145
Gerald, Joseph, 68, 90
God's Revenge Against Murder (anonymous), 86
Godwin, Fanny, 63, 65-66, 74, 124
Godwin, Mrs. Mary Jane Clairmont, 65-66, 74

Godwin, Mrs. Mary Wollstonecraft, 22, 33, 63-65, 67, 73-74, 84, 91, 99, 106, 121
Godwin, William. See separate subject entries.
Godwin, William (son), 66, 72, 74, 110
Goethe, Johann Wolfgang von, 94, 99
Goldsmith, Oliver, 38
Government, 20, 23, 25, 27-31, 36-39, 42, 44, 46, 50, 52, 60, 69, 79-80, 85, 88, 137-38, 142, 146-47
Gower, John, 132
Grenville, Lord, 60, 69, 136
Gulliver's Travels (Swift), 38, 44-47

Habeas corpus, 58
Hall, Reverend Robert, 52
Hamilton, Elizabeth, 113
Hardy, Thomas, 58-59, 69
Hartley, David, 43, 89, 143
Hays, Mary, 65, 112
Hazael (Biblical), 56
Hazlitt, William, 21, 24, 35, 40, 43-44, 51, 53, 55, 67, 84-85, 101, 124, 128, 130-31, 147
Helvétius Claude Adrien, 20, 43-44, 47, 113, 146
Herald, The, 48
Herald of Literature, The, 56
Hermippus Redivivus (Cohausen), 91
Historian, Godwin as, 22, 84, 121, 124, 128-29, 132, 141, 148
History of England, for the Use of Schools and Young Persons, The, 124, 128
History of Greece, The, 129
History of the Commonwealth of England, 141
History of the Life of William Pitt, Earl of Chatham, 85, 129
Holcroft, Thomas, 48, 55, 57-59, 70-71, 117
Honor, 46, 87-88, 107, 111, 116, 118-119, 126, 134, 148

Hooker, Richard, Bishop, 78
Hume, David, 60
Husband, Godwin as, 55, 84, 97

Imlay, Fanny, 63, 65-66, 74, 124
Imlay, Captain Gilbert, 63-64, 124
Imogen, A Pastoral Romance, 85
Inchbald, Mrs. E., 116
Independency, 42, 136, 142
Individualism, 20, 27, 29-30, 34, 37, 39, 49
Infernal Quixote, The (Lucas), 64
Influence, 84, 89, 146
Inheritance, 31
Institutes of the Christian Religion (Priestley), 57
Iphigenia, 114
Iron Chest, The (Colman), 114, 118-119
"Island in the Moon, An" (Blake), 23

Jacobinism, 62
Janeway, James, 122
Jerrold, Douglas, 145
Jesus, 36, 43, 56, 82, 136
John of Gaunt, 131
Johnson, Dr. Samuel, 35, 140-41
Jonson, Ben, 136-37
Juries, 24, 34

Kemble, John, 115, 119
Kingdom of God, 20
Kippis, Dr. Andrew, 21

Lamartine, Alphonse Marie Louis de, 99
Lamb, Charles, 19, 39, 65, 70, 113, 115, 117, 128-29
Lamb, Lady Caroline, 75
Lamb, Mary, 128
Laon and Cythna (Percy Bysshe Shelley), 75
Latin Historians, 38, 44, 47
Law, 38
"Law of Nature and Nations, The" (Mackintosh), 52
Lawrence, Sir Thomas, 59

"Letter to a Noble Lord, A" (Burke), 69
Liberty, 20, 25, 30, 36, 38, 47-48, 52, 60-61, 81-82, 100, 136-37, 142, 146
Life of Geoffrey Chaucer, 131
Lives of Edward and John Philips, Nephews and Pupils of Milton, 135
Lives of the Necromancers, 142
Lives of the Poets (Johnson), 140
Livy, Titus, 47
Lloyd, Charles, 114
Locke, John, 35, 43, 146
Lollardism, 132-34
"London Corresponding Society," 36
London Magazine, 115
Looking Glass, A True History, The, 129
"Lover of Order, A," 59-60
Lucas, Charles, 64, 114
Lyrical Ballads, The (Coleridge and Wordsworth), 91
Lytton, Lord Edward Bulwer-, 75-76

Mackintosh, Sir James, 35, 52, 146
Magistracy, 26
Malthus, Reverend Thomas Robert, 35, 52, 77, 79-80
Mandeville: a Tale of the Seventeenth Century, 101-6, 109, 126, 132, 134
Marcliffe, Theophilus (pseud.), 129
Marriage, 22, 25, 31, 33, 36-37, 40, 63, 65, 74-75, 80, 87, 96, 98, 103, 110-11, 115-16, 135-36, 146
Marshall, James, 67, 71
Marx, Karl, 145
Memoirs of an Unfortunate Young Noble Returned from Thirteen Years Slavery (anonymous), 106
Memoirs of Emma Courtney (Hays), 65
Memoirs of Mary Wollstonecraft Godwin, 64
Memoirs of William Godwin, 75, 86, 89, 101
Millennium, The, 29, 38, 48, 63, 142

Milton, John, 78, 104, 135-36, 138-139, 140-42
Misanthropy, 107, 111, 126
"Modern Infidelity" (Hall), 52
Molière, Jean Baptiste Poquelin, 124
Monarchy, 25, 30, 33, 37-38, 44, 58, 89
Monk, General George, 137
Monopoly, 25, 36, 80
Monro, D. H., 44
Montagu, Basil, 61
Montesquieu, Charles, Baron de, 89
Morning Chronicle, The, 59, 66, 105
Moses (Biblical), 136
Murder, 33-34, 76, 88-89, 111, 139
Murry, John Middleton, 32, 38, 66-67, 74, 123-24
Murry, Robert, 69

Nature of Man, The, 49, 147
Necessity, philosophic doctrine of, 22-25, 29, 42, 44, 50, 113, 125
Necessity of Atheism, The (Percy Bysshe Shelley), 72
New Annual Register, 21, 76
"New Jerusalem, The," 43, 47-48
New Testament, The, 43
Newgate Calendar, 86
Newton, Reverend Samuel, 47, 122-124, 129
Novelist, 21-22, 65-66, 75, 78, 84, 86, 90-91
Noyes, Russell, 23, 145

Oates, Titus, 138-39
Of Population: an Enquiry Concerning the Power of Increase, 79, 81
Ogilvie, James, 145
Opie, Mrs., 77, 113
Original Sin, theological doctrine of, 34, 44
Otway, Thomas, 78
Owen, Robert, 145

Paine, Thomas, 20-21, 35, 48, 51, 64, 70
Paley, William, 21

Pamphleteer, 55, 58, 60-61, 69-70, 76, 84
Pantheon: or Ancient History of the Gods of Greece and Rome, The, 129
Parr, Rev. Dr. Samuel, 35, 52, 55, 61-62, 112, 114
Particular Affections, 23, 26, 39-40, 91, 115, 120, 134
Paul, Charles Kegan, 66-67
Peasant Revolt, The, 134
Perfectibility, philosophic doctrine of, 20, 23-24, 34-36, 40, 42, 49, 70, 77, 79, 81, 95, 113, 120, 121
Peripatetic, The (Thelwall), 69
Petrarch, Francesco, 131
Philanthropy, 113, 126
Philips, Edward, 135, 140-41
Philosophes (French), 44
Pitt, William, 21, 51, 60, 69, 130
Place, Sir Francis, 68
Plato, 20, 32, 40, 104
Playwright, 22, 37, 84
Pleasure principle, 29, 31, 39, 89
Political Herald, The, 21, 76
Political institutions, 28-30
Political Justice, 21-23, 26-27, 41, 43-45, 51-52, 112-14, 116, 129, 134, 142, 145-47
Pope, Alexander, 109
Porson, Richard, 69
Positive institutions, 32
Poverty, 27, 38, 42, 68, 73, 76-77, 79, 92
Preacher, 19-20, 40-42, 55-56, 122, 127, 129-30, 139
Predestination, Theological doctrine of, 42
Preu, James Arthur, 23, 44
Price, Rev. Dr. Richard, 42, 48
Priestley, Dr. Joseph, 19, 42, 57
Priestley, F. E. L., 33, 145
Princes, education of, 30, 38, 46, 137
Private affections, 23, 26, 39-40, 91, 95, 120, 134
Prometheus Unbound (Percy Bysshe Shelley), 38, 50
Pseudonyms, 59, 124, 127-29

Punch, 145
Punishment, legal and civil, 33-34
Puritan, 42, 136

Rabelais, François, 102
Radicalism, 20, 23, 32, 36, 42, 48, 52, 60, 62, 64, 66, 120-21, 123, 145-46
Raleigh, Sir Walter, 136
Read, Sir Herbert, 145
Reason, 20, 32-35, 39-41, 43, 48, 50, 106, 120, 138, 143-44, 147
Reflections on the Revolution in France (Burke), 36, 51
Remorse, 118-20
Republic, The (Plato), 20, 40
Responsio ad Apologiam Cujusdam Anonymi (Philips), 141
Restoration, The, 137
Revolt of Islam, The (Percy Bysshe Shelley), 54
Revolution, the French, 48, 51-52, 62
Revolutionary activity, 28, 62, 69
Revolutionary War, American, 63
Richard II, 131
Rights of Man (Paine), 35, 70
Rights of women, 102
Ritson, Joseph, 69
Robespierre, Maximilien de, 52
Robinson, Henry Crabb, 51-52, 71
Romanticism, 19-20, 49, 72, 87-88, 91, 94, 99-101, 105, 108-9, 134, 147
Rosser, Henry Blanch, 67, 71
Rousseau, Jean Jacques, 35, 38, 40, 42, 44, 47, 50, 97, 108
Ruskin, John, 19

Sackville, Thomas, Earl of Dorset, 136
Saint-Simonions, 145
Samaritan (Biblical), 43
Sandemanianism, 19-20, 42, 56
Scipio, Publius Cornelius, Africanus Major, 108
Scott, Sir Walter, 103, 109-10
Seditious Meetings Act, 51

Seditious Meetings Bill, 60
Senancours, de, 99
Sensationalism, 27, 29, 34, 39-40, 43, 78-79
Seward, Anne, 115
Sermon on the Mount, 40, 136
Shakespeare, William, 94, 132, 136
Shelley, Harriet, 72, 74
Shelley, Mary, 6, 22, 54, 64-66, 72, 74-75, 82, 86, 99, 105, 121, 124, 128, 141, 145
Shelley, Percy Bysshe, 22, 38, 50, 53-54, 71-75, 84, 99, 104-5, 114, 121, 125, 145
Sheridan, Richard Brinsley, 21
Siddons, Sarah (Mrs. Henry), 115, 117
Silliman, Benjamin, 113
Sketches of History in Six Sermons, 21, 55-56
Social Contract (Rousseau), 40
Socinian Unitarian Doctrine, 19, 57
Somervell, D. E., 145
Sophocles, 118
Sothern, Mrs., 123
Southey, Robert, 48, 54, 72, 121
Spinoza, Baruch, 26, 33
Spirit of the Age: or Contemporary Portraits, The (Hazlitt), 53, 84
"Spital Sermon," 52, 55, 61
St. Leon: a Tale of the Sixteenth Century, 61, 76, 84, 90-96, 99, 103, 105, 109, 115, 126, 134
Staël, Mme, de, 99
Stapelgate, Edmund, 131
Steele, Richard, 76
Stephen, Sir Leslie, 40, 66, 125
Stoicism, 43, 83
Stuart, House of, 136-37
Suetonius, Gaius, 47
Swift, Jonathan, 38, 44-47, 102
Système de la Nature (d'Holbach), 20, 47, 57

Tacitus, Publius Cornelius, 47
Taylor, John, 69, 73
Tennyson, Alfred, Lord, 19
Tetrachordon (Milton), 136

Index

Theatrum Poetarum (Philips), 140, 141

Theism, 19, 55, 57

Thelwall, John, 35, 58-59, 62, 69-70

Things as They Are: or the Adventures of Caleb Williams, 22, 76, 84, 91, 96, 99, 103, 105, 108-9, 112-13, 115-16, 119, 126, 134

Thompson, William, 145

Thoughts Occasioned by the Perusal of Dr. Parr's Spital Sermon, 61

Thoughts on Man: His Nature, Productions and Discoveries, 32, 50, 81, 147

Titian, 91

Tom Jones (Fielding), 35, 38

Tooke, Horne, 58-60, 69

Topographical Description of the Western Territory of North America, A (Imlay), 63

Toryism, 56

Transfusion (Godwin [son]), 66

Treason, 35, 58-59, 69

Treasonable Practices Act, 51

Treasonable Practices Bill, 60

Truth, 20-21, 23-24, 26-27, 29, 31-35, 50, 62, 104, 107, 109, 111, 118, 138, 144, 146

Universal benevolence, 23, 26, 38-40, 52, 68, 89, 91-92, 95, 107, 109, 120

Utilitarian philosophy, 39, 42, 44, 109, 112

Valperga (Mary Shelley), 75

Vicar of Wakefield, The (Goldsmith), 38

Vice, 23-24, 27, 29, 33, 35, 38, 40-41, 47, 63, 79-80, 87, 108

Victorian era, 19

Vindication of the Rights of Man (Paine), 35, 48, 51, 70

Vindication of the Rights of Woman, A (Wollstonecraft), 65, 112

Walcot, John, 117

War, 30-31, 38, 79, 134

Warren, Robert Penn, 118

Watchman, The (Coleridge), 70

Watson, James, 145

Watson, Dr. Richard, Bishop of Llandaff, 56

Webb, Willis, 67

Wedgwood, Thomas, 35, 69

Wells, H. G., 146

Whig Party, The, 35, 48, 61

Wilde, Oscar, 146

William Godwin: His Friends and Contemporaries (Paul), 67

Walker, George, 112

Wollstonecraft, Mary, 22, 33, 63-65, 67, 73-74, 84, 91, 99, 106, 121

Wordsworth, William, 21, 48-49, 69-70, 91, 96, 114, 120-21

Wrongs of Woman, The (Wollstonecraft), 64

Wycliffe, John, 132, 134